Book I Evolution Series

World
Evolution

Our Future in the 21st Century

Margaret McCormick
Channel for Gunter

Channel Publishing
Huntington Beach, California

WORLD EVOLUTION
OUR FUTURE IN THE 21st CENTURY

Channel Publishing
5942 Edinger, Suite 113-130
Huntington Beach, CA 92649

Cover painting "Dawn of a New Tomorrow" Ann Van Eps

Cover design Terry Whitley

Library of Congress Cataloging-in Publication Data
McCormick, Margaret.
World Evolution: Our Future in the 21st Century / by Margaret
McCormick.
1. Spirit writings. 2. New Age movement. I. Title.
BF1301.M5 1992 133.9'3 CIP 91-091572
ISBN 0-9631930-3-1

First printing 1992
This book is manufactured in the United States of America

Acknowkledgments

I want to thank my family, my husband John for his love, support and help in making this book a reality. My daughter Laurie Mort and husband Larry and granddaughter Mindy, my son Mike McCormick, wife Toni and grandson Patrick and granddaughters Allison and Carolynn, for their love and encouragement. To my parents for providing the love and example that has helped shape the person I am today.

A very special thank you to Kathy Hawken for her continued light, support and constant encouragement.

Heartfelt thanks go to Ann Van Eps for the beautiful channeled cover painting and to Terry Whitley for the cover design.

Deepest love and gratitude to my guide Carlee and the many others for their ever present love, encouragement and help in my evolvement, which made this all possible.

Most importantly, words cannot express fully, my love, gratitude and deep appreciation to Gunter, who through his great love for all humankind has brought us this "gift of knowledge".

To all of you evolving into a new age of light, love and peace.

Author's Note

As requested by Gunter, the material in this book was written as channeled. There has been no effort made to conform to literary standards, nor make a change in the sometimes archaic use of language.

It was his fervent desire the book be straightforward, easy to read and comprehend. He explained there was a specific purpose in the use of language and the manner in which the sentences were presented, therefore what you read are his words exactly as channeled, unless otherwise indicated.

Margaret McCormick
Huntington Beach, California

Contents

Preface   I

Introduction   III

Instructions   VII

Lesson One   1

Meditation Instructions   5

Lesson Two   7

Lesson Three   11

Lesson Four   15

Lesson Five   21

Lesson Six   29

Lesson Seven   33

Lesson Eight   37

Lesson Nine   43

Lesson Ten   49

Lesson Eleven   55

Lesson Twelve   59

Lesson Thirteen   63

Lesson Fourteen   67

Lesson Fifteen   71

Lesson Sixteen   77

Lesson Seventeen   85

Lesson Eighteen   89

Lesson Nineteen   95

Lesson Twenty   101

Lesson Twenty One   107

Part II

Lesson Twenty Two   115

Lesson Twenty Three   119

Lesson Twenty Four   125

Lesson Twenty Five   131

Lesson Twenty Six   137

Lesson Twenty Seven   143

Lesson Twenty Eight   149

Lesson Twenty Nine   155

Lesson Thirty   161

Lesson Thirty One   167

Lesson Thirty Two   173

Lesson Thirty Three   179

Lesson Thirty Four   185

Lesson Thirty Five   191

Lesson Thirty Six   197

Lesson Thirty Seven   203

Lesson Thirty Eight   209

Lesson Thirty Nine   215

Lesson Forty   221

Preface

Margaret

I believe channeling is much like the meditative state, with a few differences. It takes the quieting of your conscious mind, " going within" and being "open" to receive. Many term this a trance state, which I feel unfortunately may have conjured up many negative pictures in people's minds.

It is very true that each channel's trance state will be unique to him or her. Some seem to experience deeper states than others and in my case it is very "light". To someone who does not realize, they would simply think I was in deep thought.

Learning to meditate, going within, is a wonderful way to refresh mind and body. More and more researchers are discovering the beneficial effects this has on us both mentally and physically.

There is nothing unusual or out of the ordinary about the meditative state, as we are in this state at times every day. These will be the times just before falling asleep, as we awaken in the morning, times when we may day dream, times when we are completely relaxed and enjoying some favorite activity. So you see, this is something already familiar to you. In my case, the channeling seemed to be a progression or an expansion of meditation. Each of us has this capability if we learn to use it.

My ability to channel came about through the use of meditation to reach a relaxed state of mind and body. I did not set out on a path to channel, but rather it came about gradually because of and through my use of meditation.

It is my greatest hope that you view meditation and channeling as just another of our many abilities as humans, and that you will benefit in every way from this book and the message it brings for all of us.

Gunter

As you talk with your friends on the earth plane, discussing things, learning things, it is taken for granted, you never give it a second thought.

Your teachers teach you and bring you knowledge that heretofore you have not been exposed or which requires more learning, as to the details.

This my friends is similar to channeling, except for one distinctive difference, the communication comes not from your earth plane, but from a higher dimension of consciousness.

It may seem at first to many of you, that this is impossible. After you have finished this book, if you choose to read it, you may find your thinking processes have changed in this regard.

This is altogether possible and does happen and is happening. All it takes is the "fine tuning" of your mind, letting the conscious everyday mind more or less step aside for a short time. As your mind steps aside it then allows us to communicate telepathically. Many of you may have had this happen at times you were not aware of or do not consider as such.

You were each created to do many things of which you have long forgotten and this is only one. It is a very normal, natural thing in every way. In the times to come, you as a human race, will be learning much more about this capability. At this very special time on your planet we come to bring knowledge, because as you will read further, knowledge is the key to all things.

Introduction

I am Gunter, a high teacher in my realm. I am here to impart to you knowledge of world evolution.

In the following chapters which I call lessons, I will help you understand what world evolution is and how you may begin to align yourself with the new higher energy frequencies incoming to your planet.

Before what you have termed "the fall", everyone lived in happiness, joy and love of God and all things on the earth, it's creatures, it's plant life, it's geological life. Each thing on your planet worked reciprocally, each to help the other, making one whole, one whole wonderfully working, loving planet.

You could do all things, you knew all things, and most of all you knew God. You knew God was within each and every one of you. Your powers were many and you used them with love and caring, each for the other. Life was easy, joyful, loving, all working together for each other's good.

Little by little things started to change. It was very subtle at first, barely noticeable, if you will. Some began to use their powers in a more selfish manner. They began to for-

get how important it was for everything to be reciprocal.
They became more selfish and self-centered.

As generations passed, each one forgot a little more, became a little more power hungry, a little more greedy. It
went from subtle changes at first, to flagrant changes and
attitudes and ideas.

As this happened, people devised ways, in their mind, to
manipulate others, so that they could hold power over and
control others. Because many had forgotten their own
powers, they bought into this idea and began to believe it.
They let others tell them what powers they had, and how
they were to love God and worship God.

In order to keep their power and control over people, they
manipulated and changed truths to make themselves appear more powerful. As generations passed, more was forgotten of each individual's own power. More was remembered and kept before the public notice, of the manipulated truth.

More generations passed and more was forgotten. People
became more greedy, selfish, ruthless, they murdered,
plundered, tortured. They committed every type and sort
of evil, with those that wanted to control the others, still
manipulating truths to suit themselves.

By that time, most truths as were known in the beginning,
were completely forgotten. Humanity became so evil, so
uncaring, so brutal, they were regressed to near animal
status. And yet there is always hope where God is concerned, always. He never abandons his own and an individual was sent to save humankind from themselves and
the terrible form of things they had drawn to them.

This man brought new hope to all humanity. He informed
them of the truths as they were in the beginning and
reminded them of all that they truly were. He touched
many many souls, but many could not be reached. There

was not communication, as you know it today and many refused to believe.

Because those in power felt threatened, felt he was usurping their power, he was killed, as common criminals were killed in that day, by crucifixion.

In the generations that followed, many tried to follow in this man's footsteps and live the type of life he lived, with love for others. But again, little by little, truths were changed. Again those in power, who wanted to retain power, changed truths to benefit themselves.

My friends, as you see, this has been going on from generation to generation, year to year, century to century, down through time.

When Christ the man, walked on your planet, he brought hope for a new time. He planted seeds for world evolution. Now those seeds planted so long ago are coming to fruition, in your time dear soul, in your time.

In this book, these lessons, I will explain what world evolution means to each and every one of you, what to expect and how to deal with the incoming higher energy frequencies, which will be coming to your planet.

All I ask is that you read, read and contemplate these things. If you wish to follow a path to make world evolution smoother and without incident, I have given lessons, a path to follow.

Please know that I have come at this time for this specific purpose. My Channel has lovingly agreed to allow me to speak through her and impart this knowledge to you.

I have one fervent desire and that is that you have all the information you need to make whatever decision you wish to make, this is what I am about, this is what I intend to achieve. I will be here to help until world evolution has been accomplished. This is my promise to you.

You have much help from my realm and I am but one of many.

As you read the following pages, please try to take it in as deeply as you can, thinking, contemplating and integrating. This is what I ask of you, my friend in God, this is what I ask of you.

Instructions

This book has been put together in a series of what I call lessons. There is good reason for this. I would like you to read each lesson and follow through on what I ask you to do, for one week's time. So as you can see, each lesson is for one week.

You may become impatient and feel you want to advance faster. Please try to suppress your desire to do this. I have laid this out, lesson by lesson, each one building on the other. I have done this to give you a good basic foundation.

As I will state in the lessons, the time factor of one week has to do with integrating and practicing each one of these lessons. This is of utmost importance and if you jump ahead or jump around, you will lose the effectiveness I desire to impart.

Integrate means to take the information into your being, on a conscious level, realize all the aspects of it and let it become part of you. This is at least 50% of what we are trying to accomplish.

If you follow my lessons week by week, as I have organized, by the end of this book you will have laid a good basic background for yourself, of world evolution, what it means to each and every one of you, and the steps to follow to prepare for it.

At this time I wish to thank each of you for the courage and perseverance in reading this book and applying it's principles to your life.

God bless you, each and every one, and may you begin to take on that "glow of radiance" in preparation for the time to come.

LESSON ONE

Greetings and salutations, this is Gunter. Fear not world evolution. Fear not anything, as fear will make you weak and susceptible to all type and sort of negative things. Fear opens this door and is a gesture that says, welcome negative thought patterns, you are free to enter. You have nothing to fear. What do you have to fear except fear itself, and there is no fear.

Realize you have at your disposal everything you will ever need for any situation, for any predicament, problem, anything you desire, you have the tools. You have everything within to handle any type of thing that will ever come up. Do you see how as you fear, you waste your precious energy and you change your thought patterns so that more negative thought forms can enter?

It is very important that you always keep positive thoughts in your mind. These will begin to raise your vibrations and connect you closer to God. You can accelerate and facilitate this by learning to meditate. That is a very necessary tool for you to use. That is the first tool most people learn and use in their growth.

I come to help, help you with tools for your growth. There are many people, all at various stages in their growth. There are some who have not as yet started or begun their growth process. It is those that interest me most, because I would like to help with the basics in getting started.

First there must be the desire, of course and many will have read books, heard lectures or such. They are interested and now they are at a point when they say, "I am very interested. I want to go farther, to begin to grow, but what steps do I take? What sort of pattern should I follow? I need some guidelines and some help."

Please know that help is here,
because from this day forward
I intend to help you in every way I can.

I will show you a path to follow, if you wish. I will show you ways to begin your growth, an organized way, so that you may follow this with confidence, if you so desire. Because of course, you must desire this and decide you truly want it, before you will be interested in my teachings.

I will do this through Margaret, my channel, as she has so kindly and lovingly volunteered this for the good of humankind in the transition you will all make during your evolutionary process into the time of light, love and radiance.

We will begin with the first lesson today. I would like you to begin to learn to meditate. This is the very first step in this process, to quiet your mind and free it from it's daily burdens in order to let your soul come through, in order to connect to higher intelligence, or as you call God.

In order to facilitate this I would like you to think and ponder now with me. What makes you happy? What thing or things makes you the very happiest? Think now, take your time. You may want to jot them down. As you jot them down look at them one by one and picture yourself in this happy situation. Let this feeling fully overtake you. Visualize it, feel it, let it radiate through every fiber of your being. Let it excite you, enthrall you, let it vibrate and reverberate through your being.

Take each thing separately. Do this until you "feel" you are through with that item, then begin on another. Take your time, do not hurry. Only do it for as long as it "feels" good. When the "feelings" start to decrease and ease up, stop and go to the next. If there is no next, then you will be at a stopping point.

Your mind should now be in a happy state. If you have spent some time and visualized these things, most likely you will be in a meditative state.

Now, sit quietly and notice how you feel. Notice all about it, how it feels to be happy, joyful and having and doing the things you like and want. Take a little time here and fully notice.

Now, after you have done this, realize that this is the way you bring these things about, because each starts as a seed in your own mind. Try to realize fully that you have the power to bring anything about that you want, absolutely anything. This is the power that the mind has, it always has been this way and always will, it is nothing new, unusual or out of the ordinary. This is how you were created.

The next step is to realize God wants you to use your mind in this manner. He wants you to have abundance and all that will make you happy, joyful and fulfilled. The only way you become unhappy, depressed, miserable, without what you want, is that you have pictured it this way in your mind and dwelled on it long enough to bring it about. This is true dear soul. Please see it as truth and take it into your being now.

The more you practice this exercise the more you will realize it for the truth it is. You will integrate it into your being and begin to live it, begin to be in alignment with your self/soul. As you come into alignment thus, your vibrations will begin to rise. This is the beginning.

So dear souls, for the next week I would like you to follow these procedures I have laid out for you. A summary is provided at the end of this lesson. Please do this at least once per day, at a time when it is quiet and you will have no interruptions. Next week I will expand on this with the next lesson.

Meditation Instructions

1. Think of those things which make you happy.

2. Visualize each thing, one by one, picturing it vividly until you "feel" you are done with each item.

3. Now sit quietly and let that feeling fully overtake you.

This is the meditative state.

Summary

Lesson One

1. Learn by my instructions to get into the meditative state.

2. Think of things that make you happy. Visualize them fully and with much anticipation and excitement.

3. Expect them to come about and know that you have the power to bring them about.

4. During the week, practice, set aside a quiet time each day (approximately 15 minutes or more).

5. Notebook:
   Record all the things that make you happy.

LESSON 2

After you have learned the last exercise I prescribed, the very next step is what you do after you are in the meditative state. If you have practiced like I asked, for a week, then rest assured you are reaching the meditative state and have now recognized how it feels.

Each time you begin your meditations, use the methods I have told you of, visualizing what makes you happy. Now as to what processes to use after you are in that state.

Begin by seeing an ocean. See how it flows. It flows in, it flows out. The waves wash in and they wash out. They flow continually, eternally. Now realize this is the same as your mind, it flows. Thoughts flow in and they flow out. There should be a steady flow. There should be no pressure, just a steady flow through your mind.

Picture the ocean again. See it clearly and vividly in your mind's eye. Picture it in your brain, washing in, washing out. As it washes out it takes any negativity with it. As it rushes in, it brings new thoughts, unlimited thoughts, thoughts of love, joy and happiness.

Soon, as you visualize this, you will realize that all the negative thoughts have been cleared from your mind, just the unlimited thoughts are left.

Now fully realize this, the only limits, the only limits you have, dear soul, are the ones you make for yourself. The street person fully realizes in their being, that is all they can be, at that moment. In so doing they have limited themselves to a life of misery.

A person in the ghetto sees themselves as downtrodden, befallen of life's cruelties, where only *others* have all the money and abundance. They think in terms of pennies and nickels, so that is all they will ever have, pennies and nickels, unless they change their thought pattern.

Take any man in a high position, an extremely successful position, that man wouldn't be there today, dear soul, if he hadn't thought in his mind first that he could be there. It is all in your mind.

Whatever you think, so shall you be.

It is a simple truth, but one that escapes many. Many live their whole life with limits they have made for themselves, or that others have made or imposed on them.

There are no limits, my friend, there are none, not in God's universe. For whatever you think, so shall you be and this is so. There is nothing, absolutely nothing you cannot do if you so believe. This is the truth I want to make clear to you this day, because it is one of the most important truths in the universe.

So what I would ask of you this week is, go through the lesson of last week. Get into your meditative state and go through the lesson of this week, which will be picturing the ocean, picturing it's waves washing in, washing out, taking out the negative, bringing in the unlimited. You will come to a point where you tire of this or feel that you have completed it, then at this point stop. Sit quietly, how does this feel, your mind cleared of all negative thoughts and full of ideas that have no limit? You may either visualize these ideas, or just *know* they are there, whatever they may be. Now bring it fully and completely into your being. Realize it for what it is.

You can do anything you want to do, anything, because there are no limits, only those you and others make for you. You can do anything you want to do, be anything you want to be, dear soul, by fully realizing just this one fact.

There are no limits.

So although it doesn't seem to be a week's work, it is, because most of you have been programmed differently, and I say programmed because you have taken it in and accepted it as truth. You have set your own limits and that is why you are where you are in your lifetime now, because you have programmed your mind such.

So do you see, in order to deprogram your mind, as it were, change these old habits, these limits you have set for yourself, you need to clear them out. As you do this you will then begin to see what you truly want, not what someone else wants, not what someone else tells you that you can do, but what you want and it can be anything, absolutely anything.

First you must take this truth into your being and *know* this is so, that is why we will spend a week on this. Next week we will progress further on our path.

Summary

Lesson Two

1. Follow the steps to get into your mediatative state, as listed on the Meditation Instructions.

2. Picture the ocean, washing in and washing out.

3. As it washes in, it brings positive, unlimited thoughts, thoughts of love, joy and happiness.

4. As it rushes out, it takes negative, limited thoughts with it.

5. You will come to a point where you tire of this or feel that you have completed it. At this point stop.

6. Now sit quietly, and realize fully how this feels, with only positive, unlimited thoughts in your mind. You may either visualize these ideas, or just *know* they are there.

7. Realize that is the way your mind can be at all times, because the only limits you have, are the ones you put in your own mind.

LESSON 3

It seems that many think of world evolution with fear, with dreading, with apprehension. It should not be thus, it should never be thus. It should be looked forward to with anticipation and great excitement, for this will be a time of great accomplishment for humankind.

This is the period of time so long awaited for, why would you fear this? Why would you look toward this with uncertainty and dread? There is only one answer, dear souls, and that is because you know not what to expect and that causes these feelings.

There is no need to fear, because I intend to impart to you all you will need to know of world evolution. The things I will impart to you will help you in every way and then there will be no need whatsoever for fear.

There is absolutely no need to feel thus, in fact it should be the other way around. Do you know, do you fully realize how long this event has been awaited? Thousands of years, my friends, thousands of years. So now do you comprehend how very special this time on your planet is?

It will change your way of life, forever. You will bloom as a flower, blooming in the sun of a bright new day, all will be possible for you. You will begin to use all of your faculties once again and live up to all your potential, and thus when you think of these things, think of them with anticipation and excitement.

Think of all these things that you may be able to do, all helping one another, not hating and fighting. All helping, pulling together reciprocally, one helping the other and thereby helping himself, all knowing God's great love within. This is true, dear souls. So this week, the lesson I bring you is this, one of contemplating world evolution.

Proceed with lesson one (getting into your meditative state), then to lesson two and now the following is lesson three.

Sit quietly and contemplate world evolution. Realize how very special it is, it has been awaited for thousands of years. You are here *now*, you will be here to witness this great event. Do you realize why you are there at this special time? Because you wished to be.

You came here because this was your greatest wish, to experience world evolution.

It was one of your soul's greatest desires. It is no accident you are here. You and you alone wished it, dear souls. You wished it for special and varied reasons, each one of you.

So now realize this and let it sink fully into your consciousness. You desired it, you came here at this special time for a reason and now the time is almost here. Now it is time to prepare for it so that the transition will be smooth and easily obtained.

Integrate this into your mind for this weeks's time. Let it flow through your mind and become part of you. This is yet another step of aligning with your soul. As your vibrations begin to rise, you may begin to get small glimpses of your special reason for coming. If there is none, don't concern yourself with it, but if there is, integrate it into your being. This is important that all these things become a part of you on the conscious level.

Please practice these above things for the next week.

Summary

Lesson Three

1. Follow the steps to get into your mediatative state, as listed on the Meditation Instructions.

2. Visualize the ocean and follow the exercise prescribed in lesson two.

3. Sit quietly and contemplate world evolution. Realize how very special it is.

4. Realize you are here, at this time, because this was your soul's greatest wish.

5. You came here for a special reason, each one of you, and now that time is almost here.

6. Now is the time to prepare, so that the transition will be smooth and easily obtained.

7. Integrate this into your mind for this week's time, and let it become part of you.

LESSON 4

What I wish you to do is think, think of things you like to do, things which make you happy, things of a different nature than your daily work. Whatever comes to you will be appropriate. Please write these down.

Now sit and look at what you have written down and take it in fully. What have you written down? These are things that make you happy and bring joy and happiness to your heart. Do you see how you feel? Enjoy this feeling now. This is the way you should try to feel at all times.

Thoughts of an unhappy nature should be pushed from your mind, only allowing happy joyful thoughts, in this way you raise your vibrations instantly. Do you see this? Raising your vibrations can be easy, if you simply watch the thoughts that are in your mind.

At first this may seem strange to you, different, because possibly all your life you have had a pattern of thinking that allowed all and everything into your mind. You did not cultivate your mind, so to speak.

Liken it to a garden, a beautiful garden that is tended and cultivated so that it brings forth great beauty, or one which is let go, every weed that wishes, is left to grow. There is no cultivating, no separating out of the weeds from the flowers, it appears as a mass of confusion. This is the way your mind can appear when it is left untended. Can you see the correlation?

Dear souls, this can actually be corrected easily by a little practice.

Your mind does not control you, you control your mind, for your good, for everything.

It can be used to do absolutely marvelous wondrous things, or it can be left untended, uncultivated and as such the results will follow suit.

You and you alone have the power to control your mind, your thoughts, your desires, your intentions. You are the absolute creator of your own destiny, you, not some outside force, not another person, an organization a government or a country. You and you alone can control your mind to do everything you want to do. This is how the wonder of each soul was created.

Each of you is a powerful entity unto himself, but you have forgotten this long ago, and over the ages and years most accept it as fact. But it is not fact, not truth in any way. That is one of the things I came to clear up. *This is one of the most important things you need to realize to make your transition smooth and trouble free. You must understand your own power and capabilities.* Little by little others usurped this from you. It happened slowly, subtly, a little from generation to generation, so that as time went on, it was completely forgotten and not seen as a truth any longer.

Instead people with greed and a hunger for power, in their hearts, were able to manipulate you by altering these truths a little at a time. Oh it was subtle, very subtle. So subtle that you never realized it was happening. People were able to manipulate your thoughts, change your idea of universal truths, that you all knew in the beginning, and they did so because of their own greed, selfishness and hunger for power.

This sort of thing still goes on today and you can see it's existence in some countries and some peoples. They believe what others have told them, their leaders, whether they be what is termed religious or otherwise. Do you see what they forgot? They forgot the most important truth of all.

You each have a soul and God within.

You need not look for God without. You need not follow what another man tells you is God's way, no not ever. What you need is to go within, look for God within, because that is where he is, within each and every one of you. The only step you need take is to recognize he is there, within your soul.

You are each and every one powerful entities unto yourself because each has God within him and you were created each this way, to create and do many powerful, and what you deem complex things. But you have forgotten this all long ago, buried by man's greed.

It is now time to remember all that again, to be made aware of all again as you move forward into the time of radiance. You and you alone, dear souls, have the power within you to do anything and everything you want to do.

You are completely self-sufficient, gloriously put together, you might say.

This is the truth I would like you to contemplate today, and as you do, let it fill your being with anticipation, happiness and knowing. You are a powerful entity unto yourself. You are not cattle, not to be treated as a mass. You are each powerful individuals, souls, capable of anything and everything.

My lesson for this week will be to make a conscious effort to keep negative and unhappy thoughts from your mind. It will take a conscious effort at first but as you learn to do this, it becomes second nature. Your mind learns "patterns", and if you have many unhappy thoughts continually, it is because your mind has "learned" these patterns.

So dear souls, keep on with the previous three lessons, getting into your meditative state and so on, at least once a day, but in addition to this play watchdog with your thoughts. As a negative or unhappy thought pops into your mind, replace it with a happy one, this will push the other from your mind.

As the week goes on, notice the difference it makes in the way you feel, in the way you react to others, in all ways, then next week we will discuss this a little further.

Summary

LESSON 4

1. Enter your meditative state.

2. Proceed to the ocean visualization prescribed earlier.

3. Repeat lessons one and two exercises:
   a. Think of things that make you happy and know you have the power to bring them about.
   b. Realize how it feels to have only positive, unlimited thoughts in your mind, and that this is the way it can be at all times.
   c. Know that you are each one here at this time, for a special reason, and now is the time to prepare.

4. During the week play watchdog over your thoughts. As a negative or unhappy thought pops into your mind, replace it with a happy one.

5. Notice the difference it makes in the way you feel and react to others.

6. Notebook:
   List the difference you feel it has made during the week, noting each specific item.

*You are each powerful individuals,
souls, capable of anything and
everything.*

LESSON 5

By now you should be beginning to realize several truths. You create your own destiny, you alone, no one else. It is you who is responsible for this. You may create a wonderful, loving, successful, abundant, joyful life or you may create a downtrodden, miserable, painful, pitiful, woeful life for yourself. It is your choice, dear soul, only yours.

And by the same token, at any time you may stop in your tracks and say, "Wait, I can make a better life for myself than this. It is completely within my power because I am the total creator of my destiny."

Do you see that if this were not the case, there would have been no "fall"? No, because it would have been within God's power to stop it, and yet there is the "free will" factor. You have free will in everything you do. You always have the choice, always. This is a very very potent fact to remember. You alone have all these powers unto yourself, to use for your good and other's good, but what I want to sink in fully here, is choice.

You are not coerced into anything. You may say you are and think you are, but no, you are not. You have the choice. Let us say, you have the choice of whether to accept coercion or not. Do you take in the totality of my meaning? You always have the choice.

The free will factor becomes very much a part of world evolution, because at this time there is another choice to make. Do you accept God into your heart? Do you wish to understand the meaning of world evolution and begin to make a conscious effort to raise your vibrations? These are all your choices. There will be no forcing, no pushing from this realm, but what there will be, is information so that you may learn much, and then you will have the knowledge of whatsoever you wish to do.

This is why I came, dear souls, to impart this knowledge to you, to help you realize fully your forgotten powers and the entity you really are. I will be here until this is accomplished, in other words until people have made their choices.

I know at this point you wonder, you have been told of what happens when that choice is to willingly and lovingly raise your vibrations and accept the universal truths and God into your heart and soul. But by now I am sure you wonder, what if I do not? I must know both sides in order to make an informed decision.

Up to this time, there has not been all that much written on this aspect. The reason being, we would like you to make a choice lovingly. We do not want to try to push, to coerce, to influence you with the negative aspect of it. Yet, do you not believe at the same time, you have the right to know?

I come to tell you truths, universal truths, so that you may make your choice and so that you will know the consequences of your choice either way. This is so.

My stance is thus, that I do not wish to alarm you in any way, only relate the facts and universal truths. If you make the choice not to raise your vibrations, if you say, world evolution is a pipe dream and I don't intend to go along with it because it is untruthful in it's content, remember now, you have the choice. You have the choice of books to read, channeled books from teachers such as I. You have more and more information coming from channeled sources.

You can make the decision to find out more about it or not. You can label it garbage and forget it. All I am trying to say dear friends is,

you have the choice of all these things, in every way.

We in this realm are trying to give you information just such as I am channeling now, to facilitate your making this choice.

If you choose not to participate in world evolution as such, then the incoming vibration frequencies, which will be incoming to your planet, and which will be higher with each incoming wave, will not be easy on you. Because all that will be left on your planet at the time of radiance will be those who have taken God into their heart, willingly, freely, and by their own choice.

When I say it will not be easy for you, I will try to explain somewhat without trying to alarm. If you have not aligned your frequencies, raised them to a higher vibration, and the incoming frequencies are of a certain percentage higher than those you hold in your being, you will begin to have problems in every way.

If you hold negative thoughts, these will be amplified , and by thinking negative thoughts you draw to yourself negative experiences, people and situations, these will be amplified also. Can you fathom of what I speak? If you hold happy, loving thoughts, these will be amplified causing you to go higher in your growth.

As you would draw an amplification of negative things to you, it could take the form of all sort of things and include disasters in your life, illness, pestilence, disease, I'm sure you have no trouble in deciphering my meaning. But still dear souls, at any time you would still have the choice to change, right up until the last moment, this is so. I believe I have said all on this area of the subject I care to at this time.

Many teachers have failed to bring this part up in the past, but now as the hour draws closer, it is time. Souls must know what the truths are, and I believe I am one of the first ones to impart these truths to you.

This is not to be dwelled on, only known, because knowledge is the key to all things.

If you have not knowledge, how can you make a choice of any type.

And so, the lessons I will be bringing you, are to gently and lovingly raise your vibrations little by little to help you align with your soul and with the new incoming frequencies.

This time your lesson will be to take all I have said into yourself more fully, to know these truths through and through. Practice your first three lessons and as an addition to that, while you are in the meditative state, contemplate how it will be in the time of radiance, each helping the other, each becoming awakened to their new unlimited powers. Do you find that exciting? You will bloom as a field of flowers after a gloomy day. You have so many wonderful things ahead for you, so many. Please contemplate these for the next week, until I come to you again.

Summary

Lesson 5

1. You have free will in everything you do, you make your own choice.

2. The free will factor is very much a part of world evolution as you have the choice to accept God into your heart, and begin to make a conscious effort to raise your vibrations.

3. By your way of thinking, you draw to you whatever thought forms you hold in your mind, either negative or positive.

4. The new energy frequencies, which are incoming to your planet, will amplify all, negative or positive.

5. The lessons I bring you are to gently and lovingly raise your vibrations little by little, to help you align with your soul and with the new incoming frequencies.

6. Enter the meditative state and visualize the ocean. This will be the prerequisite for all "quiet times". In so doing, you enter your meditative state and eliminate your negative thought forms.

7. Visualize what lies ahead, how it will be during the time of radiance, each helping the other, each becoming awakened to their new unlimited powers.

8. Contemplate these things this week, during your "quiet times", and at other times.

*I come to tell you truths, universal
truths, so that you may make your choice
and so that you will know the
consequences of your choice either way.*

LESSON 6

In the beginning was the word and the word was the beginning, this is what you have been taught. I will say to you now, this is a misconception.

There is no beginning and there is no end, all there is, is continuity, eternity, forever. Unfortunately there are many untruths that you have learned, learned as though they were truths because that is what was written or in doctrine of some sort.

It is now the time of remembrance dear soul. The time for you to become aware of the "real truths" that seem to have been hidden so long from you. The truths you all knew in the beginning and were manipulated and changed for other's benefits. You are a whole, all one with God.

In my realm there is no time, only eternity, forever, a continuation. Please try to realize this. You know linear time and you perceive it as such, but in actuality there is only forever. You on the earth plane are born (incarnated) live, grow old and by your term "die". It would more properly be called "pass", because you pass to another dimension. You never die, because you are forever, one with God for eternity. You perceive time, this realm has no time. We are timeless, ongoing, eternal.

After you grow to adulthood, you "perceive time passing". You perceive yourself growing older and at some point you perceive yourself ready to die. Remember that I stated, you are what you think? Remember I also said there are no limits, only those you put in your own mind? Also remember I stated what you dwell on or think, you draw to you?

Can you realize what I am getting at? You perceive yourself growing older because you perceive time. As you perceive yourself growing older, you do. Your physical body begins to break down little by little until you believe you are ready to die.

Now dear soul, whatever you perceive, whatever you think will be drawn to you and manifested. This is a universal truth and one that was forgotten and covered up long long ago. Can you see if each entity knew of their great powers, each and every one, then others who wanted to control all those entities would have a very difficult time of it.

Please realize dear souls, you had this power in the beginning and you still have this power. Nothing has changed except your perception. You don't believe you have these powers because at some long ago time someone said you didn't, someone taught you, you didn't. But that someone was human, a human who wanted you to believe this way so he could control.

Please think this over fully now. Take a look around. Look at world events and countries and leaders and peoples. Can you see that it still happens today in your own time, the telling by leaders of the mass, how to think, how to act? Do you see that over a long period of time, generation to generation, how all this becomes more distorted and more distorted. It is time for you to remember who you are and what your real powers are.

You must know the truths and remember the truths as they were in the beginning.

As world evolution draws nearer, you need to align yourself with these truths and realize your powers. You need to know these powers and the universal laws governing them.

So this will be your lesson this week. Get into your meditative state, lessons one through three, do your lessons four and five, then this lesson being six.

Contemplate your powers. Realize your powers are great, unlimited. As you do this feel a great happiness, because you are unlimited. There is no end to what you can bring to yourself, draw to you. There is no end to many other things you can accomplish, of which I will try to impart in further chapters and lessons.

You are one with God. You have God within and thus you are capable of many many things. You have been programmed, educated, taught, that you do not have powers such as these, but indeed you do.

As we continue with these lessons and chapters you will learn how to use your power in many ways that you are not familiar with. So contemplate the fact that these have been hidden from you for a very long time. Realize how this happened and why you now believe you do not have these powers, then my friend, realize fully that you do.

This is my lesson for this week, to realize that you truly do.

Summary

Lesson 6

1. You are one with God. You have God within and thus you are capable of many many things.

2. Now is the time for remembrance, to remember the powers you truly have, and what you are capable of.

3. You had these powers in the beginning and you still have them, you but need the realization you do.

4. This week, during your "quiet time" contemplate your powers. Realize your powers are great, unlimited.

5. There is no end to what you can draw to yourself. There is no end to what you can accomplish.

6. Realize these powers have been hidden from you for a very long time, and understand how this happened, and why you now believe you do not have these powers.

7. Then take fully into your consciousness that you do have these powers, to use in every way.

LESSON 7

Dear souls, I will start this by saying whatever you do, whatsoever you think, world evolution will still come about. It is something that has been coming for Eons. It is something that is coming that is natural, normal and in every way relative.

So as you can see, it is something on it's way and has been for centuries and centuries. What I want you to realize at this time, is that it is not something unusual or out of the norm. It is simply the world evolving as it was meant to do.

It will regenerate all, the whole planet, nature, creatures, souls. This is the way it was meant to be. Nature knows it is coming and will have no trouble adjusting. In fact nature has more trouble adjusting to all your pollutants such as smog and chemical wastes. It will be nature's rebirth, as it were.

Humans face a little different adjustment. You will need to start growing toward evolution as I mentioned earlier. We have covered some good basic steps so far and I hope you are beginning to see some results from this. I am only

one, one of many who come to teach. Our major purpose
at this time is to help you, enlighten you.

Now for today's lesson. Know that we are all as one,
dear souls, all as one with God. Every entity is separate
and as to themselves, but still part of a whole. This is what
I wish to speak about today.

Being a part of a whole, each one of you effects the other in some way.

As each of you thinks either negative or positive
thoughts, either loving or hateful thoughts, all part of this
whole are effected in some way.

So you see dear friend, as each person learns to love
more, learns to raise their vibration more, all of the whole
is effected. As all of the whole is effected, it helps them
think and act in more loving, higher ways.

As you work on your lessons here, as you grow higher
and raise your vibrations, you help others at the same
time. Isn't that an encouraging thought? So you not only
help yourself, you help others, because all is reciprocal.
Can you see that it keeps spreading? As each goes higher,
all go a little higher.

This is the concept which will bring about the loving
transition into the time of radiance and love. Is it not a
wonderful concept? Each helping the other and as each
does, others raise their vibrations more and more.

To help others you do not need to go out into the public
light and make a display of what you do. No, not unless
you so choose. You can sit in the privacy of your own
home and by meditating, thinking more positive thoughts,
you help the other parts of the whole without them even
knowing. This is a time when truly working together will

mean everything, because as more and more understand, change their own thoughts, it is all magnified.

This is what I would like you to contemplate and ponder on this day. Always remember the fact that you are each separate entities, but all part of the whole. All one with God and as you are, what each of you do effects the other.

Stop and think how the transition will be made into the time of radiance. It is by each and every part of this whole helping in his own way, the way that suits his personality and is compatible with who he is. Thus being so, you can see that if you have the desire to help, there will be countless ways open to you. The first and foremost starting with the basics I am teaching you here.

So the lesson this week, would be getting into the meditative state, reviewing all previous lessons and adding this one, contemplating how you are all one with God, how the transition will happen smoothly, lovingly and it will come about by all of your help and love, each for the other and for God.

Summary

Lesson 7

1. World evolution will regenerate your whole planet, nature, creatures, souls.

2. You will need to start growing toward evolution, so that the transition is loving and without incident.

3. You are all as one with God. Every entity is separate and as to themselves, but still part of the whole.

4. Being a part of the whole, what each one does, effects the other in some way.

5. As you meditate and think positive thoughts, you help the other parts of the whole.

6. The transition into the time of radiance will be made by each of the parts of the whole helping in his own way.

7. During your "quiet time" contemplate how you are all as one with God, and how the transition will happen smoothly, lovingly and it will come about by all of your help and love, each for the other and for God.

LESSON 8

We in this Realm are here to help, know that we are. We are trying to get as much information out to you, as we can, in order to make your transition process, your decision process, without stress, without strain and with love.

In order to do this, we depend on channels such as Margaret. We want each and every one of you that we can possibly reach, to get this information and have it available for them to ponder and contemplate on.

Dear Souls, you are great entities unto yourself, each and every one, greater than your mind will let you perceive at this moment. It is this we come to change and explain. You have great power, each and every one of you. As you align closer to God and the higher energies, you will be able to perceive your power more all the time. As I have said, I am one of many who come to teach, to impart this information to you.

You are what you are today, because this is what has evolved over all your lifetimes, all your many failures, successes, trials, tribulations, experiences. You, the entity that you are today, is a combination, a conglomerate, if you will, of all these many things.

Does your wisdom sometimes surprise you? If so, it is because you know many things. Your self/soul knows many things. It knows all. You must begin to make a conscious effort to let that self/soul come through in your daily life.

Let it tell you, let it lead for you, because it knows. It has had many many experiences and it knows God first hand. Most people call it intuition, but it is merely the "inner part" of "you", your self/soul coming through. Some may even call it conscience, because many times before you attempt to do something you get a feeling, sometimes very strongly, that you either should or should not do it. If it is in a quick moment, you do not have time to even think, just "feel".

Learn to trust these "feelings" more and more, because as you have no doubt noticed, they most usually are correct. Don't try to ignore them and push them into the background. Give them the credence they so clearly deserve. Listen to them, let them help you. As you learn to do this and make yourself aware of how many times these "feelings" are around, you will notice them more and more. You will become attuned to their message.

Dear friends, if you could fully fathom what powers you truly have, at this time, there would be no need for teachers and guides, none at all. Because if you fully realized, you would be different and the world would be different.

You need to fully realize how each and every one of you, no matter what their status in life, no matter what their education, no matter what the color of their skin, each and every one has more wonderful powers than they can fully comprehend at this time.

This is what you must begin to realize in the days, weeks and years to come. You must realize these truths. You must realize how you forgot them. You must realize the pattern of how over the centuries others usurped your power and told you you had none. Because as I've stated before, if you each were aware of all your powers, how could others control you?

You are made each self-sufficient, totally self-sufficient and you make your own destiny. It can be the most wonderful life in the world, or the most poverty stricken, miserable one. But you make it dear friend, you alone, by your attitudes, the way you think, you attract all to you.

This is one of the most important truths you must learn. You are the one in charge, you and you alone. Don't blame others for what befalls you. Don't be jealous of others for what they have that you do not, because you could have the same thing or more.

What way would you like to live, think now? If you could pick and choose, what would you like to do? Where would you like to live? My friends, as you think, please realize you do have the power to pick and choose, believe this, because you make and draw to you whatever you think.

You truly in every way create your own destiny.

You even pick the time you wish to pass to the next dimension. It is not some far away God that says, "It is time for you to go now". No, it is you and you alone. You create all, within and without.

Do you realize how many wars have been fought over trying to get something someone else has, when, if they had used their mind in the correct way, they would have it. There was no need to shed blood over it, inflict misery on many people over it.

Each is his own designer and creator, his own helper and healer.

This is the way you were created. This week I would like you to contemplate this fact. Sit and think quietly of it. Try to fathom what it means to each and everyone of you. Realize it is truth and just waiting to be tapped and used.

Summary

Lesson 8

1. Each and every one of you are great entities unto yourselves.

2. You are what you are today because of what you have learned over all your lifetimes.

3. Each of you is made totally self-sufficient, and is his own designer, creator, helper and healer.

4. Learn to trust your "inner feelings", because it is your self/soul attempting to lead you.

5. During your "quiet time" contemplate the fact that each of you is self-sufficient, and that you have all within to create whatever you desire. See it as truth and just waiting to be tapped.

You need to fully realize how each and every one of you, no matter what their status in life, no matter what their education, no matter what the color of their skin, each and every one has more wonderful powers than they can fully comprehend at this time.

LESSON 9

Dear souls, I believe you are at this point progressing. I believe you are beginning to experience some of the things I have been speaking of. I believe at this point you have a good knowledge of the basic things I have taught you thus far, if you have learned and integrated, as I have asked. The integration process is just as important as the learning, as stated earlier.

Dear friends, it is at this time I wish to impart to you more knowledge, other knowledge. I told you, you are all as one, as one with God. Now that you realize this, I wish you to know one more truth. By being one with God and each of you effecting all of the other parts of the whole, by the same token you may communicate telepathically with these other parts. In fact, you are already so doing, in a sense.

By the things you do and feel you send them an "impression", shall we say. They know not where this originated and they most likely think it originated with them. As you each have a connection to the other parts of the whole, so it is that you have a telepathic connection to them. As you think negative thoughts of them, they pick up this "impression" telepathically and it would work in the reverse also. So do you see, this is only more reason to "cultivate" your mind as we talked about.

For example, if you are endeavoring to deal with a person on some issue and he is being very difficult, your first reaction may be to become angry and resentful. In so doing you send out angry and resentful impressions to that person. As that person picks that up, he thinks angry and resentful things of you, which bounce back to you. Remember how we talked of everything being reciprocal? At some times this works to your disadvantage, if not used correctly.

By the above example, do you see that it tangles the web, as it were, only makes the person you are dealing with more difficult? It makes your dealing with him a compound problem, where it doesn't have to be.

Use your mind, dear souls, use your minds. That is what they are there for. Learn to use them to your advantage in every way. Don't effort and fight things, that only makes them more difficult and your life becomes one trauma after the other.

Let's face this problem in a different manner. For example, if you meet with this person and he is difficult, keep back your negative resentful thoughts. If you have a break before you meet with him again, don't let resentful thought patterns build up. Instead do your homework, which is to think good thoughts of him, loving thoughts of him. It can be done and all it takes is forming the habit to do so.

We call this "working on an inner level". You will work with this person on an "inner level".

1. Keep all resentful thoughts out. When one pops into your mind replace it with a positive thought.

2. Visualize this person and the situation. See the transaction as complete, completed to your satisfaction in every way. Do not let any other thought enter.

Now think about this. Can you see if only good thoughts are being transferred to this person telepathically, he begins to get a good "feeling" about you. It may change his picture of you. He may see you in a different light, and as such the next time you meet, he may be more willing to compromise or see things your way.

Let me tell you, when you argue, when you have a difference of opinion with another, by walking away angry, resentful and bull headed, will accomplish you absolutely nothing. It will make things more difficult in every way.

Let me ask you this, by trying it my way, what have you to lose? I would say you have everything to gain. I do not say to let another walk all over you, no, that is not my premise at all. What I do say is, stand your ground where you absolutely must. Be firm in that, but to be firm you do not need all the rest that humans most usually create to go with it.

Dear souls, life can be so beautiful, so loving, so joyful and abundant if you learn to use your mind in the way it was intended.

For so many years now it has been used incorrectly, used completely to your disadvantage and you sit and wonder why things do not work out.

Please try these things. This week try practicing this in any situation that arises, it may be business, friends, relatives.

What I ask you for this week is that you try, try for yourself and then at the end of the week you most likely will know the value of it. I will return next week with more on this same subject.

Summary

LESSON 9

1. As all of you are parts of the whole, and each of you effect the other, so may you also communicate telepathically with these other parts.

2. Learn to use your mind to your advantage.

3. As you think good thoughts, loving thoughts of a person, this is transferred to him as a "feeling".

4. As you think angry thoughts, and walk away from others, angry and resentful, it will make things more difficult in every way.

5. Learn to work with others on an "inner level" first.

6. Contemplate this fact during your "quiet time". Try practicing it in any situation that arises.

7. Notebook:
List the the situations that came up during the week, how you approached them, and their conclusions.

Learn to use your mind to your advantage.

LESSON 10

This lifetime dear souls, is different than all your other lifetimes, because in this lifetime comes world evolution. Please think and realize how wonderful this is and what an important and special thing it is to be here at this time, this time awaited for so long.

Liken this to a graduation. Humankind will be graduating to a higher level of understanding, compassion, love and abundance. At this time I would like to continue on about your powers. The powers you have instilled within you, each and every one. The powers you were created with and were forgotten so long ago.

These powers are there to help you in every way and the only thing that keeps you from using these powers, is you. You alone, dear friend, because can you realize you must believe you have these powers before they can be used? It seems such a simple truth doesn't it and yet it is absolutely what is holding you back, your realization of this.

It's odd isn't it, when you think of it. The only thing between you and the utilization of your powers, is you, you alone. Each and every human throughout your planet has these wonderful powers and yet many are in such a pitiful state, hungry, poverty stricken, ill, crippled, I could go on and on.

At any time they could stop and say, *I do have these powers. I now realize and I will begin to use them.* If they so did, immediately they would begin to pull themselves from their mire of difficulties. This is all it takes and yet it seems that this has been one of the most difficult things for humans to accept. They look for proof, when in fact if they practiced this, their proof would show itself by it's coming about. This is so dear souls.

Besides the fact that others long ago told you this was not so, you are all very wrapped up in what others think of you. In other words, going against what the majority believes, even if this is in error. Do you see the folly of this and how one person or a few persons in power can manipulate masses of people in this manner? They are told something is so, over and over again. A few begin to believe, then more. After a majority believes, if a few then begin to realize the facts they were told were wrong, they are afraid to speak up. They don't want to seem different. This is called "peer pressure" and it is a great pressure. You realize this from your teenagers. Peer pressure can do many many things.

And so to break away from the norm and overcome peer pressure, takes courage. It takes fortitude and strength. Do you fully realize though that what you will be doing at this time will effect the rest of your eternal life? When you actually stop and think on this, that is a great and important fact.

So the ones to come to the realization first, and actually put it into action in their daily lives, will need courage, because they will not be the "norm". But in so doing, they will benefit in every way. As I have told you, your powers are great and all encompassing.

As you learn to rely on your "inner feelings", as you begin to grow, you will bloom, in every way. As you do, the things you will bring about in your life, will be many and it is at that point that others will start to take notice. They will see how everything works in your life. In other words, dear souls, you will be an excellent example.

So by your example of using these powers in your daily life, you will not only be helping yourself, but others also. You will be as a beacon unto them. You will be helping them on an "inner plane" and also on an outer plane, by your example alone. This is the way world evolution will come about.

One by one by one, each awakening in their own turn, in their own way. The more that awaken, the more that will awaken.

Each person that awakens, helps the others a step behind.

When I say it takes courage dear friend, I mean the courage to stand up to your convictions on the "inner level". To know absolutely and fully you have made the correct choice and then stand by that conviction when all around you may believe differently. This is what I mean when I talk of courage.

This week I would like you to ponder and contemplate how world evolution will happen and how you will be helping others. Just by your example alone, by being aware of your powers and using them in your daily life, you become an example to others. By raising your vibrations you help others to raise theirs, because what each of you do effects the whole.

Realize fully now that your powers are only a thought away, and that thought is the realization that you have them, that they can be used for your good and every other soul on this planet. They are only a thought away.

Your life can be turned around in every way and it is only a thought away.

That is all that separates you dear friends, that is all. Please contemplate on these truths for the next week. Think fully on what I have said. Contemplate the past, the present, the future. As you contemplate these things, a realization will begin to settle within, like intricate pieces of a puzzle fitting together, the pieces of which were lost long ago. Now you have the chance to find these pieces, put them in their place and complete the beautiful picture. It is all within your power, each and every one, at this special time.

Until next week dear friend.

Summary

Lesson 10

1. This lifetime is different than all your other lifetimes, because in this lifetime comes world evolution.

2. The only thing between you and the utilization of your powers, is you.

3. To break away from the norm and overcome peer pressure, takes courage, fortitude and strength.

4. By your example of using these powers in your daily life, you will not only be helping yourself, but others also.

5. This week, contemplate during your "quiet time", that your powers are only a thought away. Ponder how world evolution will happen and how you will be helping others just by your example alone.

6. By raising your vibrations, you help others to raise theirs, because what each of you do effects the whole.

*The only thing between you and the
utilization of your powers, is you.*

LESSON 11

I have told you we are all as one, all a part of the whole and you have contemplated this. I have told you that as each of you do, effects the other parts and I have told you how all the parts are connected telepathically.

In this vein I wish to tell you of something new, something that is exciting and should be uplifting for you. Know that as you are parts of the whole and connected telepathically, you will actually be doing the others a disservice when you hold negative thought patterns and the opposite. You help others by holding positive loving thought patterns.

As this is so, I also wish to tell you that by your wanting to help others, by your wanting to help others awaken, you do so. I have told you of the energy vibrations and how as you raise your energies you will help others. Dear souls, I wish you to know as you meditate and contemplate world evolution, as you hold these thoughts in your mind, contemplating how it will be, the powers that are truly yours and how you may use them, all these things, as you contemplate, you are sending out that thought pattern to others.

They will pick this up on a telepathic level. They may not realize it at the time they do, but it will be there. It will be there as a seed which will begin to grow. You can help this seed grow in them by contemplating, meditating and thinking of world evolution.

Everything is reciprocal, that is universal law.

As you help yourself, you help others in some way, even though you may not know in what way and they may not realize it.

So by your reading of this book, and I believe you probably would not have this book unless you had been interested in this subject in the first place, as you read this book, contemplate and meditate, do all the lessons I have imparted to you, you will be helping others, because in some way they can "sense" your thought patterns.

This may not happen immediately, but the seed will be there and it will grow. Each person may be ready at a different time, it depends on many things, their lifestyle, thought patterns, personality, everything about them. As each is different in all ways, so will they awaken at different times and in different ways. Some will not awaken because they do not choose to, for whatever reason is their own.

My purpose and objective is to expose you to this information, so that you may begin thinking and contemplating it, if you so choose. Then I would like to give you direction in the form of lessons, as I have in this book, to give you a path for so doing.

I am but one of many, but heretofore there has been much written on other subjects *including* world evolution. I wish to dwell *exclusively* on this.

Please be aware that as you are contemplating and thinking you are effecting others. Someday, someway, an article, a book, may make itself known to them and they will be curious, and as they become curious and read and search, that seed begins to grow.

As you think and contemplate on world evolution, and you hold another in your thoughts, picturing him mentally, you are sending those thoughts to him telepathically. You may wish to do this with several specific persons:

1. Contemplate while meditating.

2. Picture the person in your mind, whom you wish to receive the thought telepathically.

Know that you have transferred this thought to him. You may not see evidence of this tomorrow or the next day, but done enough times, you will see evidence, dear souls, you will see evidence. So this week practice this while meditating and contemplating world evolution. Bring another into your thoughts and picture them. You may wish to do this with several people, each in turn. Bring your thoughts back to world evolution between each person, then return your mind to the next person and picture him.

Please try this. Notice how it makes you feel. Do you feel any differently? You may wish to write down notes on how you feel and what you experience.

Summary

Lesson 11

1. Everything is reciprocal. As you help yourself, you help others in some way.

2. As you read this book, contemplate and meditate, you will be helping others, because in some way they can "sense" your thought patterns.

3. During your "quiet time" practice the transference of thoughts to others:
   While contemplating world evolution, picture another in your mind, whom you wish to receive the thought telepathically. You may do this with several people, each in turn. Bring your thoughts back to world evolution between each person, returning your mind to the next person.

4. Notebook:
   List your experiences during the week.

LESSON 12

Remember how I spoke of all parts being a whole, and as they were connected, each effects the other? I wish to speak a little further on telepathy.

We spoke before of how the negative thoughts you may have for others are picked up by them and vice versa, as "feelings", "impressions". Do you realize sometime in the future you will be able to communicate through telepathy? You were created this way. You need not telephones and such because you have built within you all that you need to communicate, over miles and into other dimensions.

As I now communicate with my channel into your dimension and she into this, so can you communicate in your dimension over the miles. More and more as humans evolve, they will become aware and develop their telepathic capabilities.

The first step is in realizing they are there. Do you see that, dear souls, the first step in learning is the realization in your mind, this comes first and then the learning. Sometimes it is an experience that is simultaneous. It is of utmost importance that each person have a quiet time each day to ponder, to move and grow higher, to connect with the God within and realize their powers and the truths of the universe.

You can effect others purposely, for their good, by thinking wonderful loving thoughts of them.

This helps them in every way as they pick it up. As you think of someone and you do not get a good feeling, you get a feeling as if there were a glass between you, something stopping you, gently remove your attention from this person and to someone else or some other line of thought. This only means that person does not desire your help. He wants to be left alone. Honor this wish as each has free will and may pick and choose what he likes.

If you know a friend or relative is having a problem, in your quiet moment think some beautiful loving thought for them. They will pick it up on the "inner plane". All you do for others will return to you and as you do these things it helps all go higher. Isn't it a nice feeling to know that as you see others having problems you can help them on an inner level? There is no open display needed, you may help them anonymously. It matters not, as they will pick up this "impression", this "feeling".

As each effects the whole, each thing you do to go higher helps others. It keeps on growing and as it does and new incoming energy waves are received on your planet, the ones holding the higher energy vibrations will be capable of utilizing this efficiently more and more. As this happens more and more are awakened. Do you see dear friend how it will happen?

Those that choose not to align their energies to a higher level, will be effected more and more in the opposite manner. At the time of radiance, there will be no one left that has not aligned their frequencies to a higher level. This is so, because it will be only those who hold God in their heart, his love and his higher vibrations.

Then will be the new beginning, because once again, all parts of the whole will be working, cooperating and helping, each with the other. Your planet will begin to blossom in every way, because you will advance, quickly. You will take a quantum leap in every way.

As you look around your planet today and observe it, can you see how peoples with negative energy are drawing this to them, war, destruction, hunger, disease, poverty? My friend, this is only the beginning, because I will repeat again, all left at the time of radiance will be those aligned with the higher God energy.

This week ponder on what I have said and make a small project of trying to help others on the "inner level". Think wonderful loving things of them and let it travel to them telepathically, being aware not to intrude where a person does not desire help. See how it makes you feel. If they live in your vicinity, see if you can notice any change in them. The more you help others, the more you help yourself. This is the truth I wish you to realize this week.

Summary

Lesson 12

1. More and more as humans evolve they will become aware of their telepathic capabilities.

2. Send a beautiful loving thought to someone you know is having a problem. You will be helping this person on an "inner level".

3. As you think of someone, and you feel as if there were something stopping you, gently remove your attention from this person. This only means that person does not desire your help.

4. All left on the planet at the time of radiance, will be those who have aligned their frequencies to a higher level. Then will come the new beginning, the rebirth.

5. During your "quiet time", ponder on what I have said. Make a small project of trying to help others on an "inner level".

6. Make notes of any changes you may see in these people. The more you help others the more you help yourselves.

LESSON 13

Today I wish to work on a facet of world evolution that is sometimes overlooked.

As you are all parts of the whole and all connected and each effect other parts of the whole, so are you connected to God. You are all as one, en masse. Sometimes it is a little difficult for humans to realize this, but as you grow closer and closer to God, higher and higher, you will gain a better understanding of it.

So as you are all one, do you fully realize that God is a part of you, each and every one? He is part of you and you of him. He is you and you are he, and in so being, you might say that you are God, each and every one, because you are.

Can you fathom and realize how special this is? He is actually part of each and every one of you and you of he. Wherever you are, whatever you are doing, he is right there, right there for whatever you need.

Again I will say that the main thing that keeps people from tapping the God within, is the realization. In order to make use of something you must fully realize it exists.

At this time I wish to state, there are religions that have been very good for people and at the same time the opposite. To love God and live your life fully and to the highest, it is not necessary to follow some certain dogma, some doctrine with rules that limit all your capabilities and faculties, that ask for financial sums in order to share the privilege of attending and worshipping God.

If God created each and every one of you, and you and he are one, think now, does it make sense that you should have to travel for miles to attend some special place to contact him? I believe if you dwell on this a short while, it will come to you.

God is within each and every one of you because you are part of him.

The key here is to be aware of this, to come into the realization that this is so. When you do it will give you a completely different prospective and outlook on things.

Humans have been programmed to have shame. They have all these sets of rules and they are always feeling guilty in some way because they have not lived up to one or the other. Then it creates shame, guilt and the offshoot of that is fear, fear that they will be damned to hell forever, because that is what they have been taught or heard.

Dear soul, there is no hell. The only hell is the one you create for yourself by becoming mired in negative thoughts. As you do, you draw negative things to you and as you pass with all this negative energy attached to you, it is only amplified that much more. So if you have negative attitudes, thoughts, patterns and you pass, they will be magnified many times over. This would be your hell, if you wish to call it that.

As you realize God is there within, to help you in every way, all you need do is ask, you should feel a loving self assurance you never possessed before. You don't have to beg, pound your breast, chant or any special type of thing. Just ask and believe, and it is yours, because that is the way you were all created.

Each human, the most pitiful, miserable, wretched person, has God within and he may change his life around in a moment if he comes to this realization, and the realization that being part of God, he can do all things.

Do you believe God can do all things, dear souls? I would have to say that most of you do. Now think, if this is true, then if you are part of God it is possible for you to do all also. Wouldn't you see this to be correct? You are special, each and every one, no matter what your state, because of this very fact and it is fact and it is truth.

The sooner you can come to a realization of this and realize what it means, the sooner you will begin to use all your capabilities once more, and draw everything to you that you have ever wanted. And in so doing and realizing, your fellow human is also a part of God and to be treated accordingly, everything in your world will come around a full turn.

This week, realize these truths. Take them in fully. Think about what it means to each and every one of you and how it can change your life and in so doing, bring about the loving transition into the time of radiance.

Summary

Lesson 13

1. As you are all parts of the whole and connected, so are you connected to God.

2. God is part of you and you of he.

3. As you let these truths sink fully into consciousness, it will give you a completely different prospective on things.

4. The only hell is the one you create for yourself by becoming mired in negative thoughts.

5. Take the above thoughts in fully this week during your "quiet time". Think of what it means to each and every one of you and how it can change your life.

6. Notebook:
   Write in your notebook, ideas that come to mind, on what this very fact could do for you.

LESSON 14

Dear friends, at this point in time I hope you are beginning to realize many things, many truths that have been forgotten. This is one of the main things I wish to accomplish. Without the knowledge of your power and capabilities, you are as a fish out of water. So to be in the flow of these new incoming energies, it is vital and critical that you begin to realize these things.

Today we will begin on another subject which is also of vital importance. You must learn to "live well", dear souls. What does "live well" mean you may ask? It means to try to live the highest and best life you are capable of, during this present lifetime. The key word here is *capable*. You must learn to be *capable* of more and more all the time.

The higher you go in this lifetime, the more it will benefit your eternal lifetime.

There is a special chance, a special opportunity, you might call it, during this lifetime, my friend, and this is partly the reason you are here, because you knew this and wanted to take advantage of it. As all have awaited this special time for eons, that means each and every one of you, during this special time have what you might call, another chance, one last option open to you.

You have been working very hard over your past lifetimes to come to the point of transition, transition to the highest level you could attain. You have, with each lifetime, set out to learn what was lacking from another lifetime, some unfinished area that you wished to polish and complete. This is the reason you kept incarnating, to get to that point.

Now that point is here and at this time you will have a last choice. If you choose God into your heart and soul at this time of world evolution, you will never *have to* incarnate again. Notice I say *have to*. You may *choose to*, because you may want to live in the time of radiance, but you will not *have to*, to make up for any past deficiencies, if you choose God into your heart and soul at this time.

So in summary, there will be no one left on your planet, in the time of radiance, that has not taken God into his heart. And all those here, having chosen God, will not find it mandatory or necessary to reincarnate again. You may *choose to*, if you so desire, but it will be your choice.

The ones that have not chosen God and left the planet previously, will have a different path to follow. They have had the choice and if they choose not, there will be other alternatives open to them, because God never abandons his own. They will in some way be obliged to pick other alternatives, in order to go higher. To go higher, so that they are not left to steep in their negative energy for eternity.

This is yet another reason that this is such a special time, because you now will have the chance to break the cycle if you so desire. And again, free will is the bottom line, as you say.

It will be up to each person's own free will, what they choose.

The higher you can bring yourself, the higher you can grow in this lifetime, the more you will benefit yourselves for eternity. So learn well, dear soul. Take all that I have said into your being, contemplate it, and ponder it. Think of this special time and the special choice you now have.

Your soul knows all these things and as you align your vibrations and align yourself with your soul, all will begin to make sense to you. It will begin to dawn on you as a dream, remembered bits and pieces at a time.

But to allow this to happen, you must choose to align your energies. You must choose to learn to meditate and quiet your mind, so that you may be connected closer to God. When you do, things will begin fitting together and become clearer and clearer.

For the next week I would like you to think over this great truth, of the choice you have before you in this lifetime, how it will effect the rest of your eternal life and the things you can do towards this.

Summary

Lesson 14

1. Try to live the highest and best life you are capable of, during this lifetime.

2. You have one last option open to you, at this special time.

3. If you choose God into your heart and soul at this time of world evolution, you will never *have to* incarnate again.

4. The higher you can grow in this lifetime, the more you will benefit yourselves for eternity.

5. As you align yourself with your soul, all will begin to make sense to you.

6. For the next week, I would like you to think over this great truth, of the choice you have before you in this lifetime, and how it will effect the rest of your eternal life.

7. Notebook:
Write notes on the things you can do towards this.

LESSON 15

I wish to relate more about the same subject we have spoken of before. That is your Godliness, the God that lies within each and every one of you.

As you get quiet and contemplate, do you fully realize, fully comprehend, what this means? How this effects each and every one of you, and the belief patterns you have held in the past, and may hold in the future?

It is a wonderful exhilarating truth my friends, but it is a truth so simple and yet so important, as to change the whole world.

As you are a part of God and he of you, all things become possible for you.

This concept relates to you as no other concept could.

Up to this point, the knowledge I have imparted to you should make you feel strong and self confident. It should make you feel more in charge of your life, total control over each and every aspect of your life, because this is the control you truly have.

The knowledge I have imparted to you, is to recognize certain facts, take them into your being as truth and realize you are self-sufficient. For you are, each and every one in every way.

The more you live your daily life putting into practice these truths, the more will come to you little by little. A clarity and understanding will begin to evolve. The more you live it the more you understand. This is the way it is and will be, because you are beginning to evolve. Much like a small chick emerging from an egg.

At first you peek out at all there is outside that egg, knowing there is much, but not as yet realizing the gravity of it all, the immensity of it all. Little by little you begin to emerge, feeling your way, slowly, carefully. As you go, you become more and more confident and self- assured. With each learning experience you grow a little more and evolve, until at long last you break free of your former shackles, as it were, the thoughts and beliefs limiting you.

Just as the baby chick emerges from the egg, so do you emerge into a bright new world, a world different than it's been for thousands of years. A world where there is love, understanding, compassion, oneness with God. A time for each individual to be completely and truly unlimited, following their "inner selves" as to what they want to do and in what direction they want to grow.

Can you fathom the satisfaction, the sense of pride and accomplishment, following a path you truly love and one that you realize you can manifest in every way? It will be a wonderful time of joy and love, dear friends, and you, you there on the earth plane at this time , will witness it happening, that emergence, that evolution. You will not only witness it, but you will no doubt help bring it about by your willingness to grow and learn more and more.

This will be a time of accomplishment the likes of which you have never seen, much less imagined. For all these things to happen and come about in your life, there is one very very important factor which I wish to discuss now.

All this takes an open mind, dear soul. If you are steeped in the past, with it's traditions, it's dogmas, it's doctrines, that are thousands of years old, you will fail before you begin. It takes an open mind, a mind that is willing to "open up" to new knowledge, new facts. A mind that does not take everything at face value. One that realizes beneath each belief, each doctrine, there may lie much background, of which most of you are not aware and has all passed into history long ago and been forgotten.

Keep your mind open, letting wonderful new thoughts and knowledge flow through it.

Let it renew you, rejuvenate you. Realize the excitement and importance of this happening in your time. You will be a witness to it all, beginning right here, right now, because it has already begun.

More and more people will open and awaken each and every day, month and year. It is happening right now and all the things we have discussed in the past pages, will help bring it about, peacefully, lovingly, without incident. And so dear friend, the time comes for me to close, to bid you farewell for now.

Keep your mind open, alive, to all that is new. You will know from within what is beneficial for you. Let your "inner self", your self/soul, lead the way, because it knows all things, your past, present, future, it knows. Learn to believe in it. Learn to trust it as you were created to do. It always knows what is best for you, if you but listen to it.

Keeping an open mind is what I would like you to contemplate this week, and in so doing your "inner self" will begin to communicate with you. You will learn to trust your feelings.

This is the end of this lesson. We will continue on next week.

Summary

Lesson 15

1. As you are part of God and he of you, all things become possible.

2. The more you live your daily life putting into practice these truths, the more will come to you little by little.

3. You need a mind that is willing to "open up" to new knowledge, new facts.

4. This week contemplate an open mind, and in so doing your "inner self" will begin to communicate with you. You will learn to trust your feelings.

5. Notebook:
   During the week take special notice, to see if you have an open mind. Make notes on situations that may arise during the week. Did you follow your "inner feelings"?

*The more you live your daily life putting
into practice these truths, the more will
come to you little by little.*

LESSON 16

Please know that I am with you. I will be holding a focus for you so that you will have help from this realm, help with your understanding and comprehension of these lessons. I come to help, to impart knowledge, to show you your options. All in this realm are holding a focus for you that are desiring to grow, desiring to learn of all that is about to take place.

At this time dear friends, there are more aspects I wish to speak of, more aspects of your Godliness. You are one with God, each and every one of you.

As you work and help each other you are gaining for humanity, for humankind.

Now I wish to speak of the creatures, one and all, that inhabit your planet. These creatures will be experiencing the transition also, each and every one.

Each creature, contrary to what some of you have learned, has what you might call a soul. It is their essence, as it were, because do you see that all are one and what each does effects the other? If you are cruel to your animal brothers and sisters, it is the same as being cruel to your human brothers and sisters.

You are all as one, all meant to love each other, with each and every part having their special purpose.

Each is to help the other, and as they do, all parts work together as a perfect oneness, cooperating, sharing, each doing their part. As humans are cruel to the creatures, they are only hurting themselves, because everything is reciprocal, as I have stated.

Contemplate the creatures. What you call instincts are merely their inner self/souls speaking to them, leading them, protecting them, but have you noticed, they listen. They don't question their feelings, they act on them immediately. And yet humans who have so much more knowledge and capabilities, do not listen to their "inner feelings", because if they believe something comes not from the conscious mind, it is not to be trusted or listened to.

As you observe the animals, fish, fowl, all, you will notice how finely tuned each one is to God. As you think of this, you also realize how many times this is discussed and how humans call this instinct and assume this is the way animals are created.

Now dear soul, can you see the similarity here? You are created thus also, but you don't use it, you don't recognize and give it credence. That is the only difference. They don't question, weigh everything, try to rationalize. They act, and as you have noticed, it works very well for them. They still remain here after all these years.

Everything on your planet that is a natural (not man made) natural living thing, no matter how tiny, has some type of God essence to it. Each grain of sand, each plant leaf, each tree, each drop of water, it all has a God essence to it.

All were created to work together, each helping the other, making a beautiful, joyful, loving, cooperating whole.

Now we will speak of the plant life. Can you see what humankind has done to the plant kingdom, by their greed and wastefulness? They clear out forests that were meant to help them with watershed. They spray chemicals and pollute the air, thus harming plant, animal and human life. They are careless and unthinking, creating chemical and industrial hazards, that make it near impossible for plant life in some areas. They have completely forgotten the truths, that all were here to work together and that by so doing, all would thrive. This has been completely ignored and forgotten.

Dear friends, this must change. You have the beginnings of a change and now is the time to get behind that and carry it all the way, for a rebirth, a transition. You must realize it means a transition for your whole planet, humans, the plant kingdom, all creatures, geological life, everything. In other words this isn't just your evolution, it is your planet's evolution.

As you notice the increased volcanic activity, a shifting of the ground, seen as earthquakes, realize your planet is preparing for the transition.

So besides growing yourself and helping others to grow, you will need to make a conscious decision to help your planet in this transition.

You must see the need to stop polluting, endangering, uprooting.

You must learn to love all your creatures and your plant life and realize that as you hurt them it in turn hurts you, because you were all meant to work together in harmony and happiness, not destroy each other.

Can you see all has it's specific purpose, even the tiniest of things? Instead of realizing and looking for this, humans have attempted to make different products artificially. Can you see the folly of this? All was perfect in the beginning. What would be more useful, would be to search your plant life, your geological life, for this product, because it is there and it is perfect, because it is from God. Do you see how drugs have side effects? They are artificial aren't they, made from chemical compounds, not made by nature.

Please contemplate this week how all were meant to work together in perfect harmony, each one helping the other, each with their own special purpose.

Think of your beautiful planet and all on it. Appreciate it for what it is and begin to make an effort to change the polluting, the endangering, the destroying. If each would play some part in their own way, if each would truly realize what it was in the beginning and how each of you can change this around, then dear souls, we come even closer to the wonderful loving transition, the rebirth, the regeneration.

Think of your planet and all on it with love. During your meditative time each day, contemplate all that I have communicated to you and make a special effort to think of your planet and all on it with love.

Summary

Lesson 16

1. Each creature has what you might call a soul, their God essence.

2. You are all as one, creatures, plant kingdom, geological kingdom, with each and every part having their special purpose.

3. Each is to help the other and as they do, all parts work together as a perfect oneness.

4. What you call the creature's instincts, are merely their inner self/souls leading them.

5. Everything on your planet, that is a natural (not man made), living thing, has some type of God essence.

6. World evolution means a transition for your whole planet, humans, the plant kingdom, all creatures, geological life. It is your planet's evolution.

7. You will need to make a conscious decision to help your planet in this transition. You must see the need to stop polluting, endangering, uprooting.

8. During your "quiet time" each day, think of your planet and all on it with love. Contemplate how all were meant to work together in perfect harmony, each one helping the other.

9. Notebook:
   Write down some of the things you can begin doing to help stop the polluting, the endangering, the destroying.
   Make note of ways you can begin to use things with a God essence to them, thus fulfilling their purpose.

Everything on your planet that is a natural living thing, no matter how tiny, has some type of God essence to it.

LESSON 17

As you have thought of the animals, the plant kingdom, all the things on your planet with God essence, I hope you have begun to realize some wonderful things, some wonderful possibilities that will be available to you when you truly recognize what you are capable of.

You have read, I am sure, of people that talk to plants. Most laugh and scoff at this, yet even your scientists have found evidence that plants are living things, with their own vibrations and sound patterns. This is so because they are part of God. They are a living, breathing God essence.

Do some possibilities now creep into your mind? Dear friends, at the rebirth of your planet, so much will be possible. Think now, if you can telepathically communicate with humans and they are a part of the whole, so could you also communicate with plants. Do you realize this?

Some do it now. They may not realize it has actually been put into practice, but it has. Many speak to their house plants and they thrive. Scientists have also proven plants in a stressful atmosphere of fights and arguing, do not thrive as others do.

Scientists have found all this, yet the most important and significant part is still beyond their scope of understanding. As parts of the whole, every living thing has a God essence and because it does, and all on this planet are part of the whole, so can you communicate with plant life.

Can you fathom what this could mean in growing gardens, growing any living thing? By nurturing and love each for the other, remember all things are reciprocal, the garden would thrive. At this time think of the endless possibilities there would be. This is how it was once. You have heard of the Garden of Eden, but yet the most wonderful part of it, has not been told and expanded on.

Each living thing on your planet has a God essence and was created, each to work with the other in joyful loving harmony.

You may think this is a little "far out" at this moment, but if you contemplate it, ponder it, let it flow through your mind, more and more, it will make sense and one day a light will flash on, and the realization will come, how it makes every sense in the world.

As you treasure a stone, either made into jewelry, or just as it comes from the ground, look at it, notice it's colors, it's highlights. Is it not exquisite? It also has a God essence. Every living thing on this planet is here for a reason, to cooperate one with the other in loving harmony. This is the way it is, dear souls.

As a living God essence you have vibrations that are yours alone, individual and different than all others, and as you do, so does each God essence.

You have no doubt seen or read of how psychics find lost persons by holding something that belonged to them. By doing this, they first and foremost are "picking up" their vibrations, because all is energy at some level, and this the person is "picking up". That person's vibrations will help the psychic "tune into that person", as it were, so that he or she may be located.

I realize at this point I may have included some rather advanced information, but in so doing,

I want you to "open your minds" and realize some of the possibilities.

I want you to realize each living thing on your planet has a God essence and thus can be communicated with and this is absolutely how it was created to be.

This week dear souls, contemplate on the things I have said and let your mind come up with possibilities. If this be so, what things do you think could be accomplished? You may wish to jot these down.

This is a practice also in opening your mind, letting the thoughts and possibilities flow. How would you live? How could you improve your life by communicating thus?

Summary

Lesson 17

1. As you have thought of the animals, the plant kingdom, all the things on your planet with God essence, I hope you have begun to realize some wonderful things.

2. If you can telepathically communicate with humans, and they are part of the whole, so could you also communicate with plants.

3. As a living God essence you have vibrations that are yours alone, individual and different than all others, and as you do, so does each God essence.

4. This week contemplate all with God essence.

5. Write in your notebook:
   a. What things do you think could be accomplished, knowing that each has God essence?
   b. How would you live?
   c. How could you improve your life by communicating with the other parts of the whole?

LESSON 18

Dear friends, I hope things are beginning to fit into place. I hope many and varied things are beginning to dawn on you, about how it was in the beginning and how everything that is happening at this time is normal and natural, completely in line with who you are and where you are at this space and time.

I sincerely hope you are beginning to put these things to use in your life, and as you do, you notice the change, the change towards the positive, the change of your attitude regarding your beliefs and regarding others. As you practice these things that I have asked, I hope you see how natural it feels, because it is natural. It is the way you were created.

I realize you may grow impatient with the length of practice for the lessons. Again I would like to state, please follow what I have laid out for you. I want you to have the time to integrate and as I've related earlier, this is all important. Please try to suppress your desire to advance faster and skip around, because it will only hurt your learning experience.

As you are one with nature and everything on your planet, and you learn to work towards this direction and flow with it, everything will begin to change.

As you move along and grow and progress, you will have many insights, many new realizations.

They may pop into your mind when you least expect it. You need the integration time, it is very important and critical to the purpose.

As you see things happen in your lifetime, you will realize more and more the overall plan of things and how all working harmoniously together, can create a "heaven on earth". This is the way it all began.

Evolve and grow, dear souls. This is what it is all about. Do you realize there is never an end to growth, it goes on and on and on, even after you leave this lifetime, you will still be growing and learning?

But your lifetimes on earth have given you much much growth and experience in many things. You might want to call it well-rounded experience, because on earth you are experiencing physical matter, dealing with it's reality and learning to live and grow in this space. You have had many obstacles to overcome in your lifetimes, dear friends, many, but now you are nearing a "turning point", if you will.

Think and contemplate all your past lifetimes over these thousands of years. You have many many learning experiences behind you and now you are a maturing soul, a soul that has learned much. If you will but listen to your intuition, your self/soul speaking to you, your growth will accelerate rapidly from here on. Become very attuned to this. Give it the credence it so clearly deserves. As you have "feelings", as you "sense things", learn to believe them.

Think now of the past. You may wish to write some notes on this. How many times did you have a "feeling" about a person or situation and follow that feeling? Was it correct? How often did you have a "feeling" about a situation or person and not follow it, to then find out you should have?

I believe if you will make a list on paper, you will be shocked, because it will show you, in writing before you, that your "feelings", are correct. You have a saying, you get "good vibes" or "bad vibes" from a person or situation. That statement couldn't be more correct.

If something doesn't "feel right", don't do it.

Don't force yourself to do something that has a wrong "feeling" to you.

What I would like you to do this week, is notice, play watchdog over your mind. Write down the "feelings" "intuitions" or whatever you wish to call them. Keep a record of the "feeling" and the outcome if you followed it or did not follow it. By the end of the week I believe you will have begun to notice how many many intuit feelings you do have, and how you have repressed these in the past, not giving them any importance in your life.

Do you know one reason you don't? Because you don't know how to explain them and rationalize them, so as your civilization is wont to do, if you can't pick something apart and rationalize each and every part of it, you deny it's existence. Learn to suppress these feelings and let your self/soul communicate with you. See how accurate it is and how it always works for your higher good.

Next week we will speak of "coincidences" and how they fit in with this lesson.

Summary

Lesson 18

1. Please try to suppress your desire to skip around and advance faster, because it will only hurt your learning experience.

2. As you move along and progress, you will have many insights, many new realizations.

3. There is never an end to growth, it goes on and on, even after you leave this lifetime.

4. You are a maturing soul, one who has had many learning experiences, and are now at a "turning point".

5. Learn to suppress your feelings to rationalize, and let your self/soul communicate with you. See how accurate it is and how it always works for your higher good.

6. Notebook:
   a. Write down your "feelings", and keep a record of the outcome. How many times did you follow your "feelings"? Were they correct? Write down the situation and details.

There is never an end to growth, it goes on and on, even after you leave this lifetime.

LESSON 19

You are each and every one, capable of many many things, as I have told you and I have also told you when you realize thusly, you will achieve these things.

As you grow and learn, many doors will be open to you, doors that you never imagined would be. Each thing you learn and experience in this process of going higher and higher, will create more interest for you, so that the more you learn, the more you want to learn.

There will come certain plateaus when you feel that after all you have learned, it is only the beginning and the more you learn the less you realize you know. Both of these things are true, for as you grow higher you will yearn to know more and more, and the more you know the more fascinating it becomes.

A very important part in all this, is a quiet, contemplative, meditative time each day, to go within, to connect yourself closer to God, to contemplate the truths I have been teaching you. It is a very necessary part of the process. No matter how busy, everyone has at least one period of time per day, when he or she may do this. It will be the most significant and important part of your day. So each day as you go within, you will learn a little more, realize a little more and as you do it builds, one on the other.

You did not forget these truths overnight and so you will not remember them overnight. The meditative process is absolutely necessary to quiet your rational mind and put it in the background for a spell. As you meditate on the truths I have imparted to you, more and more will come to you. The meditative state speeds all this up. I hope you have been practicing these things in your life. This is important also, as it will show you how they work.

Dear friend, at this time I would like to tell you of your Father, the Father you left behind long ago. This Father who created you, nurtured you, was there to help in any conceivable way he could. That Father is God, the God so many have forgotten. The God that is unknown and unfamiliar to many.

He is not a God that dwells in a certain place, he is everywhere.

He is in all creation, the beautiful birds singing in the trees, the cows in the fields, the forests standing majestic and tall. He is everywhere, his love, his joy, his harmony. He is in you, waiting for you to recognize he is there. Waiting for you to realize your capabilities, your part in this planet. He is a loving God that loves eternally, who has no beginning nor no end. He can do all and as he can do all, remember your teaching that you were created in his likeness? So if that is so, you must mirror God, he is within. He does not bring accidents, misfortunes, disease, tragedy, he brings only love. You draw these things to yourself by your thoughts, because by your thoughts, you manifest, bring things into reality. You manifest, dear soul, you have this power.

To manifest is a simple thing. It is the desire and the belief. The desire of wanting a certain thing and the belief that you will bring it about. It's that simple, but you use it against yourselves, you do not use it correctly. You worry, you fret and you visualize what you don't wish to happen and as you do, you bring it about, just as surely as if you went into a store, took it off the shelf and took it home.

The sooner you realize this one fact, the faster you will progress in every way. Never, never let thoughts of things you do not wish to happen, have access to your mind. Remember how we spoke of "cultivating" your mind? Cultivate it and keep those thoughts out. *Never, never* give them credence. Visualize yourself plucking them out and throwing them away, then visualize what you want to come about.

No matter how impossible a thing may seem to attain, it is not, because manifesting is a very simple universal law.

The secret is in the realization that it is absolutely true. As I told you before about "coincidences", as you begin to manifest the things about you that you want and need, you will believe them to be "coincidences". But they will happen more and more and more.

Dear friend, nothing is a coincidence, nothing is an accident, nothing. It all happens for a special reason and it is brought about by you yourself. It is what you have drawn to you by the way you think, your thought patterns and beliefs. You may beg to differ with me at this point, but it is altogether true. It is that simple. To bring about something you must, 1) Desire it 2) Believe you can bring it about. Never, ever, let thoughts enter your head that you cannot. Can't or cannot should not be in your vocabulary. All it does is cause problems.

Begin to think of the things you want and desire, no matter what they are, no matter how unattainable you may think they are. Erase this opinion from your mind. See them as attainable in every way. Don't worry and fret about the steps getting there. Visualize your goal finalized, already manifested. Picture yourself with this manifested goal, enjoying it. "Feel" the feelings you will feel. Make it as real as you can. Do this during your quiet time each day and before sleep each evening.

The steps to get there will come, one by one by one, until it is finalized. You may say, "Oh I was so lucky this and this and this happened, just came my way. What a coincidence." Dear soul, as I stated before, there are no "coincidences", there is no "luck". These are things you have drawn to you with your manifesting capabilities. This is universal truth. Please see it as such.

Why don't you make a pact with yourself, from this day forward there is no reason to worry, to fret. Just manifest what you want, no matter what it is, it is possible. Please begin to do this during this week, while in your quiet time. The more excited, exhilarated and expectant the better and the quicker it will come about.

Until next week dear friend.

Summary

Lesson 19

1. As you grow and learn, many doors will be open to you.

2. You will come to certain plateaus, where you feel that after all you have learned, it is only the beginning.

3. One of the most important parts in this, is a quiet, contemplative, meditative time each day to go within, to connect yourself closer to God.

4. As you mediate on the truths I have imparted to you, more and more will come to you. The meditative state speeds all this up.

5. God is within each and every one, waiting for you to recognize he is there.

6. To manifest is a simple thing, it takes the desire and the belief.

7. You draw negative things to you, by holding negative thought patterns.

8. **Visualize your goal finalized, already manifested.**

9. During your "quiet time", realize fully what it means to manifest anything you desire.

10. Notebook:
    Write down your goals and the things you wish to accomplish. The more excited, exhilarated and expectant the better, and the quicker it will come about.

LESSON 20

As I told you earlier, there are no coincidences, there are no accidents. All happen for a reason and are all drawn to you, by *you*. This is true dear friends. As much as you may not wish to believe this or do not believe it, it is altogether true.

Do you realize that many times you draw your lessons to you? You may not be aware of it consciously, but you do. Your soul knows your contract, in this lifetime, as it were. It knows what you have come to accomplish, whether you realize it on the conscious level or not.

As I told you, you create, shape and form your destiny in every way. It is your making, fully and completely. There are no accidents, coincidences, good luck, bad luck, no, there is only what you draw to you, what you manifest for yourself.

Stop a moment now and look around you. Each and every thing you see is what you have manifested. You have manifested it and drawn it to you by the way you think. Those patterns in your mind that you alone can control. Others can't control your mind, even though they may think they can, or they may try, they cannot. Only you are capable of this, dear soul, that is it, only you.

So as you see, if you are the only one that is capable of this, and you draw to you what you think, then you can fully see that you create your own destiny in every way.

No one can control your mind, only you have the power to do this, you alone.

What type of circumstances are you in at the present? Are they good? Are they bad? Whatever they may be, you alone have created them, and so, as you created them, you also have the power to change them.

You manifest with your mind and as I stated before, the two essential things are the 1. Desire 2. The belief you can do so. It is such a simple thing, but as you look at your planet and see the, I will call them "downtrodden", because that is what they are, they are "downtrodden in their heart". Their life is their own making. They may be starving, ill, poverty stricken, in a moment, they can change all that, begin to grow and improve every part and parcel of their life. It will be imperative for these people to begin to realize their potential and their capabilities.

Many have gone from generation to generation, for centuries, living as their parents did, from hand to mouth. For centuries they have not grown, as far as realizing the life force that dwells within them, realizing the truths they should know in order to break the cycle.

When you stop and think of it, it's amazing isn't it? So simple a truth, so simple and yet all those long years, still not realizing, still unable to break the chains that seem to bind them.

You can help change this, dear friends, by your thoughts, by cultivating your own mind and realizing these truths and living your life to your full potential.

Whatever you want, so be it. It's that simple.

I have given you the facts, the truths, now it is up to you to bring the realization process into fruition.

Summary

Lesson 20

1. There are no coincidences, no accidents. You draw all to you.

2. Each and every thing you have, has been drawn to you by the way you think.

3. Whatever you want, so be it, it's that simple. I have given you the facts, and now it is up to you to bring the realization process into fruition.

4. This week I would ask you to contemplate the following three groups:
   a. Coincidences, good luck, bad luck, accidents, there are not such. There is only right thought or wrong thought, which brings these things about.
   b. Take a while and think of your planet and it's peoples, the people that are "downtrodden". Can you see how their beliefs, their thought patterns, have brought this about? How many have lived from generation to generation, passing these things down?

      Can you see also how some peoples have not progressed much for several thousand years? Examine their thought patterns as a whole and as you do all these things, it will then begin to sink in fully, how these things are brought about.

c. Fear is one of the most destructive thoughts there is. Learn to banish fear from your mind unless you wish to bring about that thing you fear.

5. List in your notebook:
   a. List some of what you viewed as coincidences, good luck or accidents. Then think back, can you remember the thought patterns you held at this time? Do you see how the thought patterns you held, may have brought these things about?
   b. List people you may be aware of that seem to be "downtrodden". It may be friends, relatives, acquaintances, or it may be a group or country. List any relationship you can see, between the thought forms they hold and the condition they find themselves in?
   c. Write down some things you fear. Look at them, each and every one. Beside each one, jot down what thoughtforms you held to make you feel thus. Now, realize fully how foolish it is to hold thoughts of fear, as you can draw anything to you that you wish.

   Next, write down beside each and every one, the positive thought form to counteract this.

There are no accidents, there are no coincidences. All happen for a reason and are drawn to you, by you.

LESSON 21

My friends, as we talked earlier of coincidences, this week I wish to speak to you about your truths, the truths you have so long forgotten. I seem wont to repeat this, but it is because I wish you to be so well aware of it, to focus on it, and bring it to the forefront of your life.

In the past lessons I have stated many truths and I'm sure many of them are opposed to what you have learned in your present society. What you have learned in your present society, you view as truths, yet at the same time I wish you to think on this for a moment. Most of you learned them as a child growing up and possibly some even as an adult. But where did these truths come from? They came from books, dogma, doctrine that most likely are centuries old.

I in no way mean to criticize, to ridicule your learning processes in this area. I understand what your civilization has believed for quite some time now. My primary reason for coming at this special time, dear souls, is to help you remember the truths as they actually are, not a distorted view flavored and tainted by many peoples over the centuries, who used this as a way to control the masses.

This is why I am here, to let you know the truths as they really are, what your true capabilities and powers are. As you think now, can you see and realize that if humankind had realized their powers earlier on, they would have progressed much more rapidly?

It has taken until this time, dear friends, for you to come to this point and still at this very point, a majority does not realize the full truths, their full capabilities, their purpose in the whole.

I would like to repeat again at this juncture. I did not come to criticize, ridicule, I come to impart knowledge, no more, no less, and in order to impart this knowledge, it is necessary for me to point out the fallacies in the beliefs you now have.

World evolution will happen, one by one by one. It will not happen en masse, not by huge groups of people professing to certain doctrines or dogmas. It will happen one by one by one. Because this is how it was meant to be, each person realizing at the individual level what his capabilities are, the God that is within, and the wonderful life of joy and happiness that is open to him, that was meant for him. One by one by one, each in his own turn, in his own way, in his own time.

World evolution is a very individualized thing, because that is how each person was created, to be self-sufficient,

to have all that he needed there within, to have the capabilities to handle any situation that may arise.

This realization will come in steps, dear friends, increments if you will, a little at a time. It won't be learned in one "great gulp". This is the very reason I have laid out the lessons thus, for the integration and realization to come about.

As you read the lessons and dwell on them, contemplate them for a week, do your daily meditation, you will notice all about you, situations in your life. They will serve to depict all that I have related to you, and as you do all this, the realization sinks in little by little by little. You connect closer with God, your vibrations are raised, you align yourself closer with your soul.

These are not lessons you learn by rote, one rule after the other. These are truths revealed to you, that your soul is fully aware of. These are lessons you learn by contemplating, thinking and observing the life all around you, the life of your fellow souls and the cycles of nature and your planet that continue around you every day.

There will be no tests on these lessons, no requirements of any kind.

What will come from these lessons is a knowingness. a knowingness of who you are at this space and time.

A knowingness of all about you and your part and place in it. A knowingness of compassion, love, joy, harmony, caring each for the other and all of nature.

As we are midway in this book and about to embark on a somewhat different, possibly a slightly more advanced venue, I wish you to contemplate this week the whole of what you have learned up to now.

Contemplate the difference in the way you might feel now, as opposed to the way you felt as you began this book. You may want to make a list of all the things that

have changed in your life, the ways you may have grown
and progressed, what your "quiet time" each day has done
for you, the different way you may look at the same day
to day events that occur in your life, and most of all, your
realization of the God within, that great loving energy that
makes all things possible for you.

In closing, enjoy this week.

*Acknowledge yourself for the progress
you have made thus far and begin to feel
anticipation for what is to come.*

Dear souls, we have progressed, we have learned. It is
up to you to carry this out in your daily lives and help all
others.

Next week we will begin the second phase of the learning process regarding world evolution.

Summary

Lesson 21

1. My primary reason for coming at this special time, is to help you remember the truths as they actually are.

2. World evolution is a very individualized thing, because that is how each person was created, to be self-sufficient.

3. In the past lessons I have stated many truths and I'm sure many of them are opposed to what you have learned in your present society.

4. I do not mean to criticize, to ridicule, I come to let you know the truths as they really are.

5. World evolution will happen, one by one by one, each person realizing at the individual level what his capabilities are.

6. We are now midway in this book. During this week enter in your notebook:
   a. All the ways you feel you have grown and progressed since starting this book.
   b. What you believe your "quiet time" has done for you each day.

c. The difference in the way you may look at the same day to day events that occur in your life.

Contemplate your realization of the God within and acknowledge yourself for your progress thus far.

PART II

World evolution will happen, one by one by one, each in his own turn, in his own way, in his own time.

LESSON 22

Today we start a new section of this book. The first section dealt with the beginnings, the learning to meditate, the learning about world evolution and many of the things you need to realize and do for a smooth transition. The second part of this book will go into things a little deeper, a little more advanced, you might say.

Dear friends, I hope you have seen a change in your life, a realization dawning on you about many things. As all are one, so are we in this realm part of that whole, and as we are part of the whole we are helping you in many many ways, this book being only one of many.

Already new higher frequencies of energy have come to your planet and they will increase in intensity, until world evolution is completed.

As I have stated before, the most important and critical things we come to do are: 1. Help you to remember who you are and the powers and capabilities that are your own, each and every one. 2. Steps to help you grow and begin aligning with the increase in energy. 3. To bring you information so that you may make your choice having this information at hand.

We wish to reach you, each and every one.

Each of you is as a diamond in the rough that needs polishing to become brilliant and alive with light.

We in this Realm hold much love for you, and we will be with you, helping you, nurturing you, until all is accomplished.

As you now start this second section, I hope you will acknowledge yourself for what you have accomplished thus far. It has taken a commitment to learn these things and to practice them.

As you think of your planet and all on it, please see it for what it truly is, a place of wonderful beauty and joy. Enjoy while you are there. Learn to look around you and take in each and every wonder, the golden dawn of a bright new day, the fluffy whiteness of the clouds, the drops of dew in the early morning sun, glistening as jewels.

You live on a planet that is teeming with life, wondrously alive with God essence. As you look around at all there is, realize there is God essence in each and every one of them, even the smallest most minute. They all wait, wait for your love, attention and cooperation, because all are here to work together.

As you walk in a beautiful forest, along a wave splashed sea shore, along a trail fresh with newly fallen snow, you feel alive and wonderful, do you not? It is because you are in the midst of all that God essence.

Please learn to think of these things, seeing everything alive and a part of God, because it truly is. Live each day to it's fullest, doing the best that you can do, learning to cultivate your mind and live a life full of joy and harmony. We are all as one, each and every one, all parts of the whole and our transition time is almost here after all those hundreds and thousands of years.

Learn to love your planet, your plant kingdom, animal kingdom, geological kingdom and last but not least, your fellow man. They are all one with God, each and every one.

Dear friends, this week I would like you to take special notice each day of all around you. Begin to see it in a different manner. See all in a God light and part of him. Make a special effort to enjoy your planet, to love your planet. Enjoy this beautiful place while you are here.

Do your part in whatever way you can to help your planet.

If each person helped just a little it would make a tremendous difference. This is what it takes, cooperation and all working together.

This is what I wish you to practice and contemplate this week. This will be a fitting beginning for the next part of this book.

Summary

Lesson 22

1. As all are one, so are we in this realm part of that whole.

2. As we are part of the whole, we are helping you in many ways. We in this realm hold much love for you.

3. The new higher frequencies of energy will increase, until world evolution is completed.

4. Learn to love your planet, your plant kingdom, animal kingdom, geological kingdom and last but not least, your fellow man.

5. In your notebook:
   a. In what ways do you believe you helped your planet this week?
   b. In what ways did you make a special effort to enjoy your planet?

LESSON 23

As you are all parts of the whole, but yet each an individualized person as to yourself, you seek expression, expression of the God energy inside you. As you gain more and more God energy, more and more, you will look for a place to radiate that God energy to.

As individuals, parts of the whole, you will automatically be reaching out to each other somewhat, because as I have stated before, each thing you do affects the whole.

As you raise your energy level, so will you begin to change your world, the world around you, all for the better. Things will start slipping into place more easily, without forcing, without pushing. You will be capable of concentrating more fully on one certain object, to the exclusion of others.

As you are capable of this, you will find that things may take a shorter time to accomplish, because you have focused more completely on them. As you cultivate your mind and keep the negative thoughts out and the thoughts of love and joy in, your personality, your being, will begin to radiate more love, more joy. You will find more happiness, more sense of accomplishment, in the day to day living of your life.

You are one with God and as you are, you are part of his love, his joy, his profound energy.

As your life is lived in more love and joy, you will be raising your energy frequencies.

More and more things will fit into place for you. You will begin to realize what you are truly capable of.

These things will not happen in a day, a month. They will happen a little every day, building one day on the other, one moment on the next, one week on the other. This is how your energies build, a little at a time, compounding as it were, until they are stronger and stronger, higher and higher.

You will feel the natural desire to grow, each in his own time. As you have chosen to read this book, you are reaching out, searching. You are desiring a change. This of course is the beginning, this is the way it starts, the desiring of a change. Each person will feel this desire at the right time for them. What you do with this desire, is the next step. The next step in your evolution, as it were. As each person is different, each person will react in a different way, in a different pattern.

Because you all have free will and each a different personality, when that desire appears in some form, each personality will react to it differently in his own unique way, but each will be searching.

Some may tend to fight this feeling, these feelings, try to deny that they exist, because humans have had this tendency down through the ages, this pattern of trying to deny their inner feelings, their inner urgings. They try to rationalize in every way they can and in so doing, many times attempt to repress them or fight them back.

Each has a different way of dealing with this, just as each has a different unique way of dealing with life, with anything for that matter. No two people are alike. If everyone were alike, my friends, you would have no lessons to learn, other than to overcome boredom, because it would be one huge, boring, world. But this is not the way it is, nor meant to be. Everyone was meant to be unique, each apart from the other but yet still a part of the whole.

Each of you will face evolution differently, from a different perspective, a different point of view.

What I would say to you is, to learn to trust your feelings, not your personality, not your ego, but your inner "feelings". How do you "feel" about something? Do you feel "right" about it, or the opposite? Because dear souls, those "feelings", come from within, from your self/soul.

Begin to take notice of these feelings. Try to make a conscious effort not to repress them. Let them surface, give them some credence. See what they are trying to say to you. Realize them for what they are and learn to pay attention to them, to realize they exist and notice how often they surface.

As you begin to do this, you will learn many things, dear souls, many. Just from this experience alone, you will begin to notice a pattern emerging, of how regularly these feelings, these senses, actually come through. Because after so many years of repressing them, not giving them credence, it is as though you are unaware they exist. You have learned this through a pattern of denying them existence. As you begin to notice them, you will learn many things about yourself. You will begin to realize how a pattern emerges whereby you get a "feeling" about a thing, about a person, about some option you may be considering. Let it surface and notice it and see it for what it truly is. You will notice that all along you have had this capability, this "inner sense" that may be warning you, or it may be saying to you, "this is good - follow this through".

You have called these things "hunches", "gut feelings", a "sixth sense". My friends, it is merely your self/soul sending you messages and it does this not in words, but in "feelings".

Always look within for your answers, search within and as you get quiet, contemplate and think, you will receive a feeling. Does this ring true to my very core or do I feel an uneasiness about it? Is there something not quite right about it? Never my friends, do anything that does not ring true to the core of your being.

This week will be a time of thinking and contemplating each person's personal evolution, how each will be different, just as each person is different and unique. The most important thing is to go by your "inner feelings", what "feels right" to you. Because the ego, the personality, the rational mind, may throw all types and sorts of conflicts and ideas at you, ideas of a negative nature. Ideas that tell you not to give credence to your feelings. But in parting, I will say your "inner feelings" are from your self/soul, that God part of you. I believe more need not be said.

Summary

Lesson 23

1. As you change your energy level, so will you begin to change your world.

2. As you cultivate your mind, you will begin to radiate more love, more joy. You will find more happiness, more sense of accomplishment in the day to day living of your life.

3. Each of you will face evolution differently, from a different prospective, a different point of view.

4. As your "inner feelings" come through, make a conscious effort not to repress them, give them credence.

5. Always look within for your answers. Never do anything that does not ring true to the core of your being.

6. During your quiet time contemplate your own personal evolution, how it will be different than all others, because each person is different and unique.

7. Notebook:
   a. Jot down what you believe were ideas and conflicts your rational mind, your personality, cast at you during the week.

b. Beside each one, record if this was recognized and dealt with at that moment, or at a later time.
c. By the end of the week were you having greater luck recognizing these things and dealing with them?

LESSON 24

This aspect has to do with you, you alone, you and all that you are. I will say the totality of what you are. You have dreams, you have desires, and these dreams and desires are the seed. The seeds that will grow into reality, if you in fact nurture them and hold them in your mind in the right way.

Manifesting means bringing something into reality.

It begins first with the thought in your mind, because everything that you bring about starts with a seed in your mind first.

If you become aware, aware of how your mind works, aware of the capabilities you have, that you are not now putting into organized use, you can draw to you exactly what you want. You may think this sounds too good to be true, but it is the absolute truth. This is universal law, always has and always will be. It is there for you to make use of in every way, for your every good.

*You have been using this skill even
though you were unaware of it, because
this is how all things come about,
through this very principle.*

As I believe I have stated before, as you look around,
and as you see people in the ghettos, poverty stricken
people, the type of help these people need most of all is
to educate their minds. To educate their minds in the way
of universal law, manifesting law, because the reason they
are where they are is due to the fact they cannot visualize
and believe they can be anywhere else.

Do you see the violence, the gang wars as you call
them? These are people who feel trapped, trapped in their
own mind. They have taken their mind and molded it,
molded it and put all type and sort of limits up.

In their own mind they see themselves trapped in this
way, trapped in their "place in life". *They* feel as though
all the "privileged" people, as they would call them, have
it all. *They* have it all and they want to keep it all. *They*
don't *want* the "ghetto person" to have anything. They
don't care about his wants, his desires, his hunger, his
poverty.

Thus, they adopt an attitude of "we are against you and
everything you stand for", because we will never have it.
You have it and you won't share, and you don't care how
miserable we are. And in so thinking, they imagine the
"privileged" persons being responsible for it all.

As they think this, they feed on it, one to the other, and
as they feed on it, it grows, because remember, everything
starts as a seed in your mind and as you think and dwell
on it, you draw it to you. Hate builds and as it does, all

the rules of the "privileged ones", as they see it, are flaunted, are purposely broken, killing, robbing, plundering.

As a way out many turn to drugs and the "easy money" they see from drugs. Just another way to say, "I don't have to follow the rules you made. I'll break each and every one of them." In drawing more and more to themselves, they lose all track of any value except the negative, which grows worse and worse.

Dear souls, what these people need is a reeducation, a reeducation of their mind, so that they may realize how it works, and that all can be theirs if they use their mind in the correct way, the way God meant it to be used. They are trapped in their own mind. They can change their way of thinking and change their entire life. This is all it takes pure and simple.

I have used the above to illustrate a point. A point that is a little drastic in this case, but no less a point. As you think, so shall you be. This is absolutely how it is and this is one of the most important truths to be learned.

You are capable of controlling your mind in every way. You are the creator of your destiny in every way.

Each soul on this earth has the power and capability to raise themselves to any status they so desire.

This is the way they were created. This is the very most important thing to integrate and realize.

Whatever you desire, no matter what, can be brought about, by you, dear soul. You can do it by your way of thinking. You can manifest what you want, and the higher your vibrations, the quicker you manifest. It is as simple as that.

This week I would like you to think over the things I have said. Let it integrate into your being. Think of it and realize how true it is in every way. During this time think of the things you truly want, no matter what they are and as you do, let yourself begin to feel an excitement, an anticipation, because they can be yours and you have the power within to bring them to reality. Next week we will expand on this, with manifesting lessons, so to speak.

Summary

Lesson 24

1. Manifesting means bringing something into reality.

2. If you become aware of how your mind works, you can draw to you exactly what you want.

3. You have been using this skill even though you were unaware of it, because all things come about through this principle.

4. You are capable of controlling your mind in every way, and *as you think, so shall you be!*

5. The higher your vibrations, the quicker you manifest.

6. During your "quiet time" contemplate the principle of manifesting. Visualize the things you would like to manifest, and let yourself begin to feel an excitement, an anticipation, because you have the power to bring them to reality.

7. Notebook:
   Make a list of the things you wish to manifest. Add to them during the week, if you think of more. This will help you keep these things in the forefront of your mind, during your "quiet time".

*You can manifest what you want, and
the higher your vibrations, the quicker
you manifest.*

LESSON 25

I come to impart knowledge, knowledge for all humankind, to help in your transition and your progression toward the evolution of your planet.

I am here to help, to nurture, to be of service in any way I can. As you read my words, please know that I am with you. As you read and have the desire to grow, know that I am there to assist you with these processes.

As I have so often told you, I come at this special time, for just this purpose. To grow spiritually first takes the desire. The desire to learn more, to know more. The more you learn, the more is your desire to learn. It is as a seed that grows within, a seed nurtured by your learning, your pondering, your searching and putting into use what has been learned.

Desire is a great thing, a wondrous thing and from desire all things are born.

Think on this a moment, is this not true? Desire begets all things.

As you have learned, for something to come about, it must first be a thought in your mind and that thought, dear friends, is a desire, a desire to grow spiritually, a desire for a material object you wish to draw to you. It all starts with desire. The more burning the desire, the more clearly you can picture the desire, the more quickly it will be brought about. This is nothing more than universal law at work.

There are certain known laws within the universes, and this be only one, but it is a powerful, yet simple one. It sounds simple, does it not, and it is, but yet it eludes many, because they have not come to the realization that it is so.

You must realize to the core of your being this is so. You must take it in for the truth that it is, a magnificent and powerful truth.

It will serve you in every way. It will change your life around. It will draw all to you that you have every wanted, if you but take it into your being and realize it.

It is so simple and yet so powerful, it eludes the majority who look for proof, endless explanations and recitals. As I have imparted to you before, if you but try it, put it into practice, the proof would be forthcoming.

Dear souls, you will come to a point in your growth, upon reading of a certain truth, immediately you will recognize it within. It will strike you somehow, that this is so, and at the same time feel very familiar. This is the way spiritual growth unfolds. The searching, the finding and the knowing. Your soul recognizes these things.

If you have the desire, if you are searching and looking, you will find.

It will all open to you as a flower opening, petal by beautiful petal. Each opening in it's turn and exposing itself to the bright rays of the Sun.

As your path, if you will, your life, unfolds little by little, it will be enlightened with the rays of God's love and light, warming your heart and soul and helping, encouraging you on your way, ever onward and upward. Desire, the burning desire for a "thing", material or spiritual, is the vehicle that will bring it about.

As we speak of manifesting, this is what it takes, the burning desire. The "feeling" of this desire, intently, all consuming. The more of this "feeling" you have and the higher you have raised your vibrations, the sooner these things will come about.

So this week I would like you to spend some time thinking of your life before you. What a wonderful life and opportunity it is, in this time you have left on the earth plane, there is so much you can do.

At this time, during this week, begin to think of what you *really* want out of the balance of your life. As you think, don't effort or force your thoughts, just let them flow into your mind. Some may come at unexpected times, while working, playing. Write them down.

Then as you look at them, more or less prioritize them. This one will probably come first and then this and so on. Take whichever one that may have the top priority on your list and during your daily meditation, begin to picture it. Visualize it, as on a screen in front of you. It comes in from the left and leaves to the right, much as a picture slide.

See it as already manifested and you using it or being included in some way in the picture. As you do this, spend some time on the "feelings" you will have when this is manifested. "Feel" them as completely as you can.

Next week we will travel this same road further.

It will all open to you as a flower opening, petal by beautiful petal. Each opening in it's turn and exposing itself to the bright rays of the Sun.

Summary

Lesson 25

1. I am here to help, to nurture, to be of service in any way I can. Know that as you read my words, I am with you.

2. Desire begets all things. For something to come about, it must first be a thought in your mind, and that thought is desire.

3. To grow spiritually first takes the desire, the desire to learn more, to know more.

4. The more burning the desire, the more quickly it will be brought about.

5. You will come to a point in your growth, upon reading a certain truth, immediately you will recognize it within. This is the way spiritual growth unfolds.

6. This week spend some time thinking of your life before you. Begin to think of what you *really* want out of the balance of your life. As you think, don't effort or force your thoughts, just let them flow into your mind.

7. Notebook:

   a. Write down these thoughts as they come into your mind.
   b. Prioritize them, according to your wants and needs.
   c. During your daily meditation, begin to visualize the top item on your list, as on a screen in front of you.
   d. It comes in from the left and leaves to the right.
   e. See it as already manifested and you using it or being included in some way in the picture.
   f. As you do this, spend some time on the "feelings" you will have when this is manifested. "Feel" them as completely as you can.

LESSON 26

Today we will speak a little further on coincidences. As I have explained to you before, there are no coincidences, because everything is brought about and manifested by you.

You create your destiny, your reality, your all, so do you see, dear souls, the things you call coincidences are not that at all. They are only what you have drawn to you in one form or the other.

When you manifest and you desire a specific thing or result, then you must be specific in your manifesting visualizations. Let me give you an example. If you wish great abundance in the form of money and visualize it as such, possibly yourself surrounded by money, the money will be forthcoming, but you have not specified in "which manner" you would like to make this money. Because you have not been specific and because you have not focused intently upon which way you will accumulate this money, it could come about by many means. My advice is thus, the more clearly, intently, you can picture a specific thing, the quicker it will be brought about. In other words the example I have given above is like the cart pulling the horse.

Know your definite desires thoroughly.

So let's go back dear friends, and take that example again in a little different way. Instead of picturing the money, which you know you want as an end result, visualize the means you would wish to take to get there, such as, a business you would love to be in, a job you would love to have, or possibly several things. Remember, there are no limits, only those you put up yourself. You are your own creative person and you will think of many different ways, each of you, and this is how it should be, because you are all unique unto yourselves.

The more specific you can get, the easier it will be for you to visualize. The easier the visualization, the easier for you to "feel" the feelings that go along with those visualizations.

I would suggest you make an outline, a chronology of sorts. You may start out and desire point A and point B. Under point A and B in chronological order, list the steps necessary to bring this about. There may be only one step or there may be many, you will know.

Keep this list, this outline. Each day in your quiet time, one of the things you will do is visualize what you are desiring to manifest. When this comes about, your manifestation is complete on that certain subject. Mark it off your list.

You will be amazed, for as time ticks by and passes, you will find that one by one, you are manifesting the things you desire.

Your rational mind may immediately come to the decision that this is "just coincidence", but as you go on, more and more, you will realize it is not coincidence at all.

You, my friend are drawing these things to you. You are creating and manifesting the things you want by your visualization, your way of thought.

These thought forms will project themselves out into your world, drawing these things to you.

As you check more and more off your list, you will begin to realize fully and consciously, that you indeed can create any reality you desire. You can prove this to yourself, just by putting these methods into practice.

At this point I need to add a couple of things. Keep negative thoughts out. I can't say this emphatically enough. If you try to visualize during your quiet time, but the balance of the day allow negative thoughts regarding this subject to enter and take hold, you will defeat your very purpose. If negative thoughts creep in, pluck them out, throw them away and then place a positive thought or visualization in it's place.

To visualize during your quiet time and then the balance of the time, entertain negative thoughts, is self defeating. Remember the dominant thought prevails. If it is of a negative nature, so be it. If it is of a positive nature, so be it.

Look around you at this moment. All, absolutely all you have around you at this very moment, you have drawn to you. You have the power to do this. If there are situations, relationships, material things in your life that you don't

find to your liking, remember, in some way, you have
drawn these to you. On a conscious level you may not understand why or how, but you have done it yourself.

*Any situation you wish to change in your
life, anything, can be changed by your
thinking, manifesting processes.*

You dear souls must realize how powerful you really
are.

So this week, make your list. Define your desires and
the steps to get there. Add to your list whenever you want,
but with each desire, begin by visualizing the first step to
getting there, if there be one.

Summary

Lesson 26

1. There are no coincidences, because everything is brought about and manifested by you.

2. When you desire to manifest a specific thing or result, you must be specific in your manifesting visualizations.

3. Rather than visualizing the end result, visualize the means you wish to take to get there.

4. Keep negative thoughts out. If you allow negative thoughts on the subject to enter, the balance of the day, you will defeat your very purpose.

5. If a negative thought enters, pluck it out and replace it with a positive thought.

6. Remember, the dominant thought prevails.

7. Notebook:
   Make a chronological outline of each thing you desire.
   a. List the goal, or the object of your desire.

b. Under each goal, list the steps, one by one, you feel necessary to bring this about.

c. Begin, each day during your "quiet time", to visualize the first step under each goal.

d. When this comes about, mark it off your list, and go to the next.

You are creating and manifesting the things you want by your way of thought.

LESSON 27

To manifest, I have given the steps of desire, visualization and "feelings". There is one more very important step that you should be aware of. It is love of self.

Love of self may sound out of context here, but it is not, because many many people never "make it", because they lack self-love.

To put this in another way, they feel they are not deserving of these things. On one hand consciously they may want something, desire some certain thing very much. Their desire may be very strong. They may visualize well and have the right "feelings", but unless they have love of self, and feel also that they deserve these things, they will not manifest them, or manifest much slower.

Dear souls, you must have self-love for many reasons.

To be enlightened, to grow, to bloom, you must have love for self.

You cannot love others completely when you know not love of self.

You deserve every abundance and happiness in your life, each and every one. This is your universal birthright. As I stated before,

God does not want you to suffer. He wants you to be joyous, happy and filled with love for all, including yourself.

To grow, it is imperative to have love of self.

How can you love others if you do not love yourself? Remember you draw all to you. You make your own reality, so if you don't believe you deserve something and at the same time you are trying to manifest by visualization, "feelings", do you see you do nothing but throw yourself into chaos? How can you manifest something you actually feel you don't deserve? Many people are like this. They have not self love.

So at this point during your quiet time, think on these things. Do you in your opinion, feel you deserve all the good and abundance in life? See what comes through when you ponder on this.

Do you do nice things for yourself, ever, or do you do it all for others? Do you put others needs, wants and desires before yours always? If this be the case, it is most likely you feel this way.

To grow and become a strong entity unto yourself, you need to realize that you deserve love and abundance as much as the next person. It is your birthright.

If you come to the conclusion you do feel this way, you need to correct it. This is a two part process.

First, contemplate what has caused this. Most times it has to do with patterns and thought forms that were programmed when you were growing up.

You may have been treated in this manner by someone who induced guilt in you. You were made to feel shame or guilt for things you did. Try to trace this back and begin to realize where it came from.

Many people grow up this way and it "cripples" them for life, because of course, if you feel inwardly that you do not deserve, then of course is it not logical that you will not receive? After you have traced this and feel you have pinpointed how it came about, you are ready to rid yourselves of it.

Secondly, realize this can be changed. You do deserve everything good in life. That is how you were created. Not being deserving is a fallacy, it is not true nor ever was.

During your quiet time picture yourself as being deserving and loved, loved by all and especially yourself.

Love yourself for what you are, a unique, loving human being with the capacity of great love and the capability to bring into reality all you have ever wanted.

As you love yourself it ripples out to others in every direction. So, as we spoke of all being parts of the whole, dear souls, as you love yourself, love is radiating out to others.

This week I would like you to:

1. Contemplate and see if you feel that you have love of self. If you decide you are lacking in this area then go to number 2.

2. Contemplate during your quiet time what has caused you to feel thus.

Thirdly, when you pinpoint the cause, erase it. Face it head on and see it for what it really is. Picture it as a symbol of some sort. It is there in your being, now pluck it out and throw it away, get rid of it. You may want to picture yourself burning it. Whatever suits your taste and makes you feel very definite about disposing of it.

Picture a beautiful ray streaming downward from above. It is a ray of hope and love. This ray is bright and brilliant and it enters the empty space left, and fills it. That space is now filled with God's love and light. From this day onward you will love yourself, for you are worthy and deserving of all that is good.

If you feel you do not have a problem in this area, spend this week reinforcing it, realizing how as you love yourself, you in turn radiate out to others.

During these processes I would suggest writing these things in your notebook. Writing them also has an impact on your mind and makes you more aware of them. You also thus, have a record for further use or reference.

Summary

Lesson 27

1. To manifest, you must have love of self, and feel deserving of that which you wish to manifest.

2. To be enlightened, to grow, to bloom, to love others completely, you must have love of self.

3. You cannot manifest what you feel you don't deserve.

4. You deserve love and abundance, this is your birthright.

5. As you love yourself, it ripples out to others in every direction.

6. During your "quiet time", contemplate, do you feel you deserve all the good and abundance in life?
   a. If you do not feel deserving, ponder what has caused this. Trace it back and begin to realize where it came from.
   b. Realize this can be changed. Not being deserving is a fallacy, it is not true nor ever was.
   c. When you pinpoint the cause, erase it. Picture it as a symbol of some sort. It is there in your being, now pluck it out and rid yourself of it.

   d. Picture a beautiful brilliant ray streaming downward from above. It is a ray of hope and love. It enters the empty space left and fills it. That space is now filled with God's love and light.

   e. From this day onward you will love yourself, for you are worthy and deserving of all that is good.

If you have not the above problem, spend this week reinforcing it, realizing how as you love yourself, you in turn radiate out to others.

7. Notebook:

   a. If you do not feel deserving, write down each reason. You may come up with few reasons, or many.

   b. They may come at various times during the week, which will necessitate your adding them to the list.

Writing these things has an impact on your mind and makes you more aware of them

LESSON 28

You are all at a cross roads of sorts. You are suspended between the old, on the one hand, and the new on the other. You are at a juncture, dear souls, a point in your life where you will exercise your free will. Do I embrace the old, the familiar, and continue on as before, or do I take a step forward to the new, the uncharted, the unknown?

Do I take a step forward in my spiritual growth and reach upward more and more toward God, more and more toward his light, his love, his oneness? Do I evolve and continue evolving along with the planet, or do I choose to hold onto the old, the familiar? This is all up to you.

It is a very big step for some and not as much for others, because you are each unique, but all the same it is a juncture, and you will choose one or the other.

As you have read and practiced and meditated on your lessons, I have been there to help, to help you integrate, realize and understand what I have stated in these lessons. But in the end, it is up to you alone. You alone have the power to choose whatever you may wish.

You may not choose now, you may wait and read more books, search more, question more and this is as it should be, because each of you will come around in your very own time and when you do, and if you do, you will know at that moment, exactly, completely, this is what you want. It is a two part process.

First comes the searching and questioning and then the decision.

The decision may come to you, each of you, in many ways and at many different times.

You will not begin your search unless you have the desire to begin with. Usually the more that is read and understood, the stronger that desire becomes, until you are satisfied within and without, then comes the decision.

It is not a choice to be made out of fear, fear of what is to come in the following days, months and years.

It is a decision to be made out of love, love for God and love for self.

If it is made out of fear, dear souls, you will not grow spiritually, you will not progress. But on the other hand, if you fear enough to stop and search within, it may be the dawn of your spiritual evolution.

Anything done from fear, entirely, is completely self-defeating. Fear is one of the most harmful thought forms that you have, dear friends. As I told you about "cultivating" your mind, you should learn to overcome your fears. To fear is to plunge yourself into negativity and despair. If you let fear take precedence over all else, you will find that you are in a mire that will only increase unless you change it.

As I told you earlier, as the increased energy frequencies reach your planet, there will be an increase in the intensity of whatever state your mind may be in.

If you hold fear and hatred in your mind, it will be intensified. Do you realize and see that if something is intensified, such as fear and hatred, it is only more difficult to lift yourself back up?

As you hold love in your heart for God and for your fellow souls and all nature, these feelings will be intensified.

You will think in higher ways and as you do, more will be revealed to you consciously.

More and more, you will understand how it all fits together.

This week I would like you to contemplate on fear. As you "cultivate" your mind, make very sure you keep fear from it. There is nothing to fear dear friends, as all can be faced head on and worked through, step by step, with love and harmony. As you fear, you draw to you the very thing you fear.

Keep notes in your notebook. What fears have you had during this week? Write them down. Why do you have that fear? Try to pinpoint a reason or reasons that you have it. Many times while doing this, it becomes clear to you how senseless this fear really is.

Pluck it out and rid yourself of it. If it arises again, you may want to reread your notes and this will reaffirm your realization of the senselessness of it. Then pluck it out again.

Never give it credence and never let it remain, because if you do, it will only grow, slowly, becoming larger and larger.

Realize fear is like a cancer. It may begin small but it grows slowly, spreading it's ugly tentacles, taking over.

Listing the things you fear will also help you be aware of the "type" things you fear, and solutions may come to you during your quiet time.

Realize that your fears are completely without merit due to the fact that you alone create your own reality, you draw to you what you think. Contemplate this and realize how foolish fears really are.

1. They mire you deeper and deeper in negativity.
2. They do not solve any problem.
3. They bring about exactly what you are fearful of.

Summary

Lesson 28

1. You are at a crossroads of sorts, suspended between the old, on one hand, and the new on the other.

2. You are at a juncture, a point in your life where you will exercise your free will.

3. Do I evolve and continue evolving along with the planet, or do I choose to hold onto the old, the familiar?

4. It is not a choice to be made out of fear, but out of love.

5. Anything done from fear is self-defeating. Fear is one of the most harmful thought forms there is. As you fear, you draw to you the very thing you fear.

6. The increased energy frequencies reaching your planet, will intensify whatever state your mind may be in.

7. During your "quiet time" contemplate how foolish fears really are. Realize that your fears are completely without merit due to the fact that you alone create your own reality.

a. They mire you deeper and deeper in negativity.
b. They do not solve any problem.
c. They draw to you exactly what you are fearful of.
   Solutions may begin coming to you during this time.

8. Notebook:
   a. Write down the fears you have during the week.
   b. Below this, list the reasons you believe you have this fear.
   c. Pluck it out and rid yourself of it.

   Listing what you fear will also help you be aware of the "type" things you fear.

LESSON 29

I am a being of light in my realm. It is more correctly called a light body, for it is made up of much energy, a personality within a light body, you might say.

Our energy is vast and powerful, it takes into consideration all things. We can manifest immediately at this level. As we think, so it is. This is true, it is thus because of our concentrated energy and the frequency of our vibrations. And so as you raise your frequencies more and more, you will manifest quicker and quicker. This is the way it is, dear souls.

I realize I have spent quite some time discoursing on manifesting, the reason being that it is imperative for you to understand this thoroughly. Because when we speak of manifest, we speak of bringing something into reality and that something may be material, a situation, a relationship, an event. So you can see if it be thus, how very important it is for you to understand and digest the concept.

There are no limits, only those you put in your own mind. We have discussed this often also. As I spoke earlier of focusing on your goal in steps, in order to be more specific and to bring it about quicker, there is yet another aspect to this.

You may have an end goal in mind. It may be rather large and you may have only partial ideas of the steps to take. At this point, you will focus on that end goal and as you do each day during your quiet time, the steps will open to you, one by one.

So in this case, the importance would be to focus on your end goal and when you do, know, be certain the steps will be forthcoming, and they will. Be prepared for them to come in many different ways and forms, because if you have not been specific, you may be somewhat surprised at times. It may not happen as speedily as when there are specific steps taken one by one, but there is absolutely no doubt, you will get there.

Focusing intently also helps speed up the process. The more intense the "feelings", the clearer you visualize and take into consideration the smallest details, the more times you focus, such as twice or three times a day, instead of one, the quicker it will come about.

There is one other situation, of which I would like to speak. If you have chosen to help others in this lifetime, as an example, helping humanity understand and prepare for world evolution, in other words, if your goal is to benefit many people, for humanities higher good, then dear souls, look for your manifestation to come about very quickly and easily.

If you know not the steps, but have the fervent desire, the steps will unfold before you, each in it's proper turn.

Besides using your own powers, you will tap into many others also.

We in this realm are seeking to aid all humanity at this time. If you have this fervent desire, the rightness of purpose and intent, dear souls, the accelerated pace at which you will grow and manifest everything you need for this purpose, will amaze you.

Just by having the fervent desire to help humanity and work toward that goal, will raise your vibrations immensely. As you can see, it all goes hand in hand. We are seeking those that will help us. The time approaches near, we need to accomplish much.

For those who seek to help, there will be no obstacles.

Manifestation will happen quickly, completely and your goal will be brought about more easily and more swiftly than you ever dreamed possible. All things will open to you and what you need and want will be there.

So, in your weeks's contemplating and quiet time, think all these things over, how manifesting is accomplished and what your place is in this.

Some people may desire to manifest mainly for themselves and a mate or partner, some mostly for family. It is universal law and as such, there are no limits. But as soon as you have the intent of helping many others and humanity, as a whole, your growth and manifestation will accelerate in every way.

Contemplate all these things during this week. Things may begin flowing into your mind as far as things you want to do and have, and to accomplish.

Write them down in your notebook. Contemplate your place in the universe, what a truly wonderful planet you have and how all things are possible. Integrate this fully and completely and realize what it means to you, each and every one.

Summary

Lesson 29

1. As you raise your frequencies more and more, you will manifest quicker and quicker.

2. If you have an end goal in mind that is rather large, and only partial ideas of the steps to take, you will focus on that end goal, and as you do, the steps will open to you one by one.

3. Focusing intently helps speed up the manifestation process.

4. If your goal is to benefit many people, for humanities higher good, look for your manifestation to come about very quickly and easily.

5. During the week:
   a. Contemplate how manifesting is accomplished and what your place is in this.
   b. Contemplate your place in the universe, what a truly wonderful planet you have and how all things are possible.
   c. Realize what the above means to you, each and every one.

6. Notebook:
   Write down all the ideas that come to you, on what you
   want to do and accomplish.

LESSON 30

At this space and time, you should be realizing many things. If you have followed along with these lessons, as I have asked, your integration process should have been very good and complete.

As I have mentioned, more than once, this is at least 50% of the process. It takes the pondering, the thinking, the contemplating, and as you do, you will also have many insights during your quiet time.

As I have mentioned, we in this realm want to help each person that begins this path of learning. Know that you are one of many on your planet at this time, searching, reading, learning and integrating. You may read different books, be at different levels, in your learning process, but the one thing you all have in common, is the subject, God and world evolution. People from all walks of lives, people in different areas of your planet, are searching and learning, as are you.

As you contemplate during your quiet time, think of these others. Visualize all connected, one to the other. As you learn and integrate, you are getting brighter and brighter, more filled with light and love.

If you will notice, there are many trying to clean up your
planet, learning to recycle and reuse and care for your
wonderful planet. More and more you and others like you,
will begin to realize the God essence in nature.

You will begin to see and to learn the
harmony and love of cooperating with
nature, yielding more food than ever
before.

You will learn that chemicals, man made chemicals, are
not the things your plants and gardens thrive on, they
thrive on cooperation from you. A working with them,
providing them the things with God essence they need to
produce their fullest bounty.

In the past you have viewed all as separate, plants,
animals, geological life, even your own body, completely separate from your mind and soul. But dear friends, it
is all as one, all parts of the whole and as such each part
seeks love and cooperation from the next, in order to
achieve his highest potential.

In the past there has been a chaos of sorts, because many
times all parts were working against each other. If you
had been "tuned in", so to speak, with the other parts of
the whole, you would have known what they wanted and
needed.

As soon as humankind can realize and take in what this
means to each and every one of them, the sooner your
planet will thrive again, much like the Garden of Eden of
old.

The Garden of Eden is but a name, a name given to a
period of time when all on your planet lived and worked

in harmony, one with the other. They realized the rhythm and harmony in all things. They knew the God essence in all things. The more awareness you have, of all the above, the quicker will your planet make it's transition, along with you, smoothly, peacefully and without major incident.

Have you ever noticed how there seem to be cycles for everything, winter, summer, spring, floods, droughts, childhood, adulthood? This is how it was meant to be, each thing in it's own time and place, all blending one with the other to create your beautiful planet.

Whatever each and every one of you can do, however small, will be a big step toward the healing and rebirth of planet Earth.

Each effort you take toward recycling, purchasing in different ways, supporting groups that are helping, will be a step in the right direction, a step closer to evolution and rebirth. As you look at your trees, your greenery and gardens, see them for what they truly are, each having a loving God essence, each a part of the whole.

I would like you to ponder nature this week, mainly your plant kingdom. During your quiet time, contemplate how even the minutest blade of grass, has a God essence. It is a living, breathing thing of God.

Write down some ideas of what you can do to cooperate and be more in tune with your plant kingdom. If everything in the plant kingdom has a God essence, what difference would this make in your world, your life?

Make a conscious effort to begin in your own way, to recycle, save resources and clean up your lovely planet.

List the things you did during the week and the things that you would hope to do from this day forward. All it takes is a little effort on the part of each.

Summary

Lesson 30

1. As you contemplate during your quiet time, think of the others on your planet, searching, reading, learning and integrating.

2. Visualize all connected, one to the other.

3. The quicker you view all as one, plants, animals, geological life, souls, and not as separate, the sooner your planet will thrive again.

4. As you look at your trees, your greenery and gardens, see them for what they truly are, each a part of the whole.

5. This week:
   During your quiet time, contemplate nature, mainly the plant kingdom. Realize that even the minutest blade of grass has a God essence and is a living breathing thing of God.

6. Notebook:
   a. If everything in the plant kingdom has a God essence, what difference would this make in your world? (list)
   b. Your life?

   c. Write down some ideas of what you can do to cooperate and be more in tune with your plant kingdom.

   d. List the things you did during the week to help recycle, save resources and clean up your planet.

   e. What things would you hope to do from this day forward?

LESSON 31

You are one unique person, whole and self-sufficient within yourself, yet still a part of the whole. You have a part of you that lasts through eternity. That part, your soul, remembers all about you. It remembers all your past and it knows the future.

Your soul is your "whole you" if you will, because it will continue on after this lifetime, just as it has, after other lifetimes.

It has been learning, experiencing, growing, until it is what you have within, at this moment. It knows all, it sees all, whether you are consciously aware of this or not. The "feelings" that come from within are from your soul, let's call it your self/soul.

Your self/soul always tries to protect, to lead you in the right direction, on an upward growth pattern.

As you read and hear things, you may get a "feeling" from this self/soul, a definite feeling that "senses" certain things about what you read or hear.

You may read a passage and in a "flash" of shall we call it "felt/sense" you "feel" it ring true to your very core. This will depend on many things. It will depend on 1. How open you are to receive 2. Whether you will admit and give this felt/sense credence.

As I have stated before, many times you try to repress these feelings. You have developed a pattern of this, due to the fact you have programmed yourself this way.

As we also spoke of before, you need to become consciously aware that you have these "feelings" and that they come through every day of your life. They are there to guide you, to help you, but this will not happen unless you recognize them for what they truly are.

You have a saying, "I'll sleep on it". This is a very wise choice, when you are trying to make a decision, because in your sleep, your dream state, which is but merely another state of consciousness, you will be more free to take into consideration all sides of your problem. It will have no interference from your rational mind.

During your dream state, you are in a state of consciousness, which is more or less timeless, in touch with the universe and in touch with your soul.

In your dream state you process many things, you know many things. To "sleep on" something overnight, will give this problem, this decision, over to your self/soul and it's connection with the universe.

As you wake the next morning, you may "feel" an instant answer. Do not expect this answer in words, expect it in "feelings". To let this answer come through in feelings, you must be willing and open to let your feelings come through. And so you see, the past exercise I gave you of recording your feelings, noticing them, giving them credence, is for a specific important reason.

The other thing I wish to speak of is openness. By this I mean the ability to have an "open mind." Dear souls, let me explain a little further on what my meaning of an "open mind" is.

To have an "open mind" is to not label everything immediately as it comes in.

Many have preconceived ideas, ideas they have programmed themselves with over the years. It has somewhat to do with negativity in some ways.

Immediately they put a label on something that they hear, they read, if they have never heard this is so and the "mass mind" (by mass mind, I mean the majority of the public), does not believe it, they rule it out. They rule it out as not being true or possible. This also has something to do with peer pressure. The "mass mind" and peer pressure are intertwined and interrelated.

To have an "open mind" is to hear or read an idea, not label it immediately, to let it flow through your consciousness, taking time to let your self/soul give you a "felt/sense" about it.

I will say at this juncture, many people seem to be this way by nature, their personalities. It has to do, many times, with the way you were raised and formed your thinking patterns when small. It also has to do with your spiritual self and how developed and how your spiritual feelings are.

If you look within and are truthful with yourself, you will know if you have a closed mind or an open one.

Just because you may have a closed mind, doesn't mean you cannot change it. You can make a conscious effort, when you hear something or read something, to not make judgement on it immediately. Let it enter your mind and flow through it. Repress your feelings of judgement and as you might say, "sleep on it awhile".

The second part of this would be to pay close attention to your "feelings" after this. Remember to give them credence. Let them arise and see them for what they are, your self/soul giving you an answer. Again, it will not come in words, but through a "feeling".

This week dear friends, I would like you to practice this. Upon hearing or reading something, make a conscious effort not to "judge" this thought. Let it flow through your mind and then see what "feelings" surface regarding it.

Keep notes on this. Write the things down and write what feelings "come up". Pay close attention. Learning this is a very important part of your growth process, as you will be allowing your self/soul to guide you. Your self/soul who knows all and has your "higher good" in mind always, not only throughout this lifetime, but through eternity.

Summary

Lesson 31

1. Your soul is your "whole you", because it will continue on after this lifetime.

2. The "feelings" that come from within are from your self/soul.

3. Your self/soul always tries to protect and lead you in the right direction.

4. To have an "open mind" is to not label everything immediately as it comes in.

5. You can make a conscious effort, when you hear something or read something, to not make judgement on it immediately.

6. Notebook:
   a. Practice making a conscious effort this week, not to judge something immediately, upon reading or hearing it.
   b. Let it flow through your mind and write down what "feelings" surface.
   c. At the end of the week, look at your list and then make your decision.

d. Were any of the decisions different than you would normally make?

LESSON 32

Dear friends one and all, you are each and every one a part of God and he of you, and by that token, you naturally have pure love in your heart, because God is love.

Even the most despicable, what you may call, evil person, on the earth plane has some speck of love in him, because he is part of God.

What is up to you, completely, is to what extent you will grow during your lifetime, how much you will "allow" that love to grow. How much you will nurture it and search out more information in order to learn more about God and his ways, about his love.

As your birthright is also free will, which each and every one of you have, you have this choice. This choice to seek further, to let this love grow and nourish it with every possible bit of information, experience, compassion

for others. This is your choice, yours alone. No matter
what someone may subject you to, they cannot take away
your free will.

As I mentioned earlier, the "free will factor" is what
caused the "fall", because at that time you did not choose
God. You did not choose to let his love grow, to nourish
it, to become more fully a part of him.

No matter what you did, God did not forsake you. How
could he forsake his own? He could not. He was always
there and if you chose to turn to him, at any moment, at
any time, he was there for you. For he was always there,
a breath away, within your very heart and soul.

At this special time you have the choice again.

This time I hope you will read, search, contemplate
what all this means in your own life. To choose God, to
choose to let that love within you grow, will benefit you
in every way. It will benefit you now, in this lifetime, and
it will benefit you in your eternal life.

I have imparted to you information that many may not
be familiar with. Much are things long forgotten, there on
the earth plane. Although they have been long forgotten,
your soul recognizes these truths, it recognizes everything
about them. So as you read and learn about these things,
underneath, just below your consciousness, you already
know them. In other words, in a different state of consciousness than your every day waking state, you are well
aware of these truths.

You are a many faceted entity, with many many parts
to you, if you will. You may see yourself as "you", the
physical body and believe that is "you", but you have

many more parts than that. You are multi-dimensional. That means, dear souls, you are capable of living in many dimensions, many consciousness at the same time.

This may be a little difficult for you to fathom and understand. It is not something to worry and concern yourself with, because little by little, the more you choose to grow, if you do, it will all fit into place.

The choice to grow, if you choose to grow, is yours alone.

No one can force this on you. It must be your own conscious choice.

As you began reading this book, you may have read books on this subject before. On the other hand, you may have never read anything on this subject before. My fervent hope is that you followed the book, the way it was laid out, so that integration and learning went hand in hand, one with the other.

At this time you should be approaching the decision you will make, or I might rephrase that, as you have taken the information in, it is as though on a scale in your mind. The scale is probably weighted more in one way than the other, so that your decision may not be made yet, but you have gained many opinions and ideas.

I have purposely written this in a way to make you think, to think creatively, to use many of your creative thought processes that you may only use on occasion. You need this exercise, you need to begin using these faculties, that so many do not now put to use.

God has great love for you. I and those in my realm have great love for you. We all desire to help. If we didn't we would not be bringing information of this type through for you. You are unique and special, each and every one.

This week I would like you during your quiet time, to visualize your planet. See it as you might from outer space, and as you do this, visualize a network, a network of humanity all connected, one to the other. You may picture it as dots of light, all connected by lines of light, it makes no difference. What does make the difference is that you picture it in your own way, and as you do, picture it connected to a network in our dimension.

Each of you may see this and picture this a little differently, and that is no matter. The picturing and visualizing is the important thing.

We are all as one, all of you in your plane and all of us here. All as one.

As you do this, you will "feel" a oneness with God, a oneness with your fellow souls and all of humanity.

This is what I wish to impart to you this week, the feeling of oneness, oneness with all.

Summary

Lesson 32

1. Even the most despicable, evil person has some speck of love in him, because he is part of God.

2. It is up to you completely, to what extent you will "allow" that love to grow.

3. At the time of the "fall" you did not choose to let this love grow, to nourish it, to become more fully a part of him.

4. During this special time, you have that choice again.

5. During your "quiet time" this week:
   a. Visualize your planet. See it as you might from outer space. As you do this, visualize a network, a network of humanity all connected, one to the other.
   b. You may picture it as dots of light, all connected by lines of light, it makes no difference. As you do, picture it connected to a network in our dimension. You will "feel" a oneness with God, a oneness with your fellow souls and all of humanity.

6. Notebook:

Write notes of any special feelings that surface this week.

LESSON 33

Dear friends, the time is now, now to practice your lessons and raise your vibrations. With each passing day, the time of radiance approaches, closer and closer. All is being readied with great care, love and joy. We need your help, each and every one of you, to help the evolution of your planet happen, smoothly and without incident.

We in this realm can only do so much. We bring you information and help in any other way that we possibly can. In the end, it is your planet, your life and your free will. You will read, search, ponder and at some point make your choice.

I want to remind you, that whatever your choice is, God is still with you, because he is with and within each and every one of you. He will never forsake you. Those of you who may not wish to grow spiritually, who may not choose to take God into their heart at this time, you are not lost. No one is ever lost, no matter what his deeds or actions.

The difference at this point will be the road that you travel. Let's put it this way, one will take the high road and one will take the low road. There are no in-betweens involved here, not in the end. There is but a choice of aye or nay.

My purpose has been to try to let you see the many facets of it, present the information for you to contemplate.

Since you have begun this book, you have progressed greatly, you have been presented with the universal truths as they are. I have attempted to lay out lessons in such a fashion that you will have time to think, ponder, run it all through your mind and integrate.

I have come to you, because I have great love for you, for all humankind. You are as a brother or sister, in my eyes, and it is my fervent desire to help you at this special time. If you were in my realm and could look out on all of humanity and see the goodness, the love, caring and rightness of purpose, that was there, it would warm your heart, as it does mine.

Yes, there do exist peoples who may not be *as* loving and caring as others, but that does not mean they are without love. Everyone has love within, because they have God within and God is love. As I stated last week, it depends on you whether this love will increase or decrease. This is completely up to you in every way. For the love to increase, you first need the desire, as I have also stated earlier.

You on the earth plane at this time are very special to us. This time has been so long awaited and now it is here. It is such a special time and the reason you are there, now at this time, has much significance.

Whether you realize it consciously or not, it is so. You chose to come here at this time, each for a reason of their own. Although you may not realize consciously, your soul knows, it fully knows why you are here and what you came here to accomplish.

As I also stated earlier, listen to your self/soul. Let the feelings come through and give them credence, because it is trying to lead you in the direction and path you came to accomplish. The more you listen and give credence, the more your mind and heart will open to the God within. A step at a time it will unfold, until you see quite clearly why you wanted to come at this time.

Happiness, abundance, joy, can be yours in every way, when you learn to live your life in the way of universal laws and truths.

This is so, dear soul.

I have asked you to open your mind to all, allowing all thoughts to have entrance, no matter what. They can be discarded later, if you feel them not appropriate, but give them a chance. Don't push them out because you have read it is not so. Don't push them out because you are told it is not so.

Do you realize the greatest inventors of your time, Edison, Alexander Graham Bell, had an open mind, completely without limit? How many times do you think they were told, "it can't be done"? But they went by their feelings, because deep within they knew it could be. They gave those feelings credence. They allowed them to stick

around. They allowed them priority over what others told
them and they read.

Do you think that when Galileo told all that the world
was round, that he was believed? Up until that point
everyone thought the opposite. All books taught it to be
the opposite, but he persisted. It all started with a "feeling" and an open mind in which he allowed this "feeling"
to come through and he acted on it. This is true.

If you think back over your history, you will begin to
realize how many great men, came from their "feelings".
They did not go along with the "mass thought" of their
time. They had the individuality to think for themselves,
to follow their own "inner feelings", even though the
majority were not in agreement.

*It takes inner strength which comes from
God's love and light, to live your life in
this manner.*

To live your life in the way "you" see fit, to do what is
best for your higher growth.

There is a special reason you are here, dear soul and this
week during your quiet time, I would like you to contemplate this. Write down what thoughts may come to
you. Don't force or push, don't be impatient if nothing
much comes, just be open to receive. That is what I am
asking. Until next week.

Summary

Lesson 33

1. We need your help, the help of every one of you, to help the evolution of your planet happen, smoothly and without incident.

2. There are no in-betweens here. There is but a choice of aye or nay.

3. I have come to you, because I have great love for all humankind, and it is my fervent desire to help you at this special time.

4. You chose to come here at this time, each for a reason of their own.

5. It takes inner strength, which comes from God's love, to live your life in the way "you" see fit.

6. This week contemplate during your "quiet time" on the special reason you are here.

7. Notebook:
    Write down the thoughts that surface during the week. Don't force or push, just be open to receive.

If you think back over history, you will begin to realize how many great men, came from their "feelings".

LESSON 34

There are many in your world today who have love for their fellow man, who are beginning to realize somewhat, in their own way, the course events seem to be taking. They seem to have an inner "feeling" that you are all on the "brink" of something, on the "brink" of something new, something that will effect all mankind.

They have this "feeling" and it comes from deep inside. Some may not recognize this "feeling", may not even realize it is there, or they may "realize" it at moments, fleeting moments now and then. They have these "feelings" because their soul knows. Their soul knows why they came, why they are here at this special time. Their soul is trying to tell them, let them know, as it were. As each is in a different stage of progression in their growth, some will realize much more than others.

One of my many purposes for coming, is to help you realize what your soul is attempting to tell you. You may have realized, have had a feeling, there is something new adrift, something new in the wind. Some of you may not have recognized that you have these feelings at all.

Take this time now to do a little exploring. Think and contemplate this last year, for example. Just do this easily and let the "feelings" and thoughts flow through your mind.

Have you noticed any differences between this past year, from other years for instance? Do you notice any difference in your "feelings" about situations, goals, people, the world in general?

Do you feel impatience with people of a negative nature, more so than before? Do you feel dissatisfied with your goals, your present employment, possibly things you have done for years, now somehow seem "not quite right"? Dear souls, this is your soul trying to tell you something. It is trying to do many things at this time and it needs your conscious help.

As I asked you earlier to keep track of your "feelings" in a notebook, I would still like you to do this. Now as you do this, you may want to begin categorizing these. They may fit into certain categories, of which you may make a title. Date them and keep track of them day by day. You will begin to recognize a pattern. The "feelings" come under certain categories.

As you do this, don't fret, don't overly concern yourself with these things, just get them down and categorize them. Then contemplate them, easily, gently, try to decipher what they are trying to tell you.

As new waves of energy reach your planet, there are many things that will be happening. You may become dissatisfied with certain things you have been doing for years, but you know not why.

You may feel a burning desire to do something special in your life, but you know not what. You may feel bored with things that in the past held great interest for you.

You may be more interested in the world and world affairs. You may feel something is lacking in your life, but you cannot seem to put your finger on it. Sometimes it seems just beyond your grasp. Dear souls, many of you are going through this now, some more than others. It is for a reason. It is your soul attempting to jog your conscious mind into paying attention to it, it is attempting to help you remember your reason for coming at this special time. What I wish to do is help you to realize and recognize this. Keep your notes in your categories, and little by little you will begin to make sense of these "feelings".

There is one important thing I will say to you.

Whatever is not relative to your higher growth and path, whatever it may be, will become more distasteful to you.

You will seek more and more those things that tend to make you happy and alive in your day to day life.

It will be up to each person to sort out his own purpose, why he came, what he wants to do, and the number one priority here is to keep listing your "feelings" in categories, in a notebook each day.

This I do not want you to approach with impatience, forcing, pushing, but instead with a joyful attitude, happiness and with love in your heart. In other words, don't force your mind, just let it flow and write it down, that is all I ask of you dear friends. Don't be overly concerned that you will have the answer tomorrow, or the next day, or a week from now. Just let it flow and get it down on paper.

At some point it will come to you, what it is that you want, what direction your soul is leading you in. Just be patient and let it unfold before you. Be open to receive, be open and give the feelings credence and write them down. At some future point it will come to you, and when it does, then comes the manifestation.

I have taught you, the steps to manifest what you desire. As you find your "path", then you have but to manifest this and bring it into reality.

This week begin keeping these notes in categories and prepare to make this a continuing project in your life. It only takes but a few minutes, yet it will reward you with the answers you are seeking.

Summary

LESSON 34

1. Some in your world today, seem to have an inner "feeling", that you are all on the brink of something new that will effect all mankind.

2. One of my many purposes for coming is to help you realize what your soul is attempting to tell you.

3. As new waves of energy hit your planet, you may become dissatisfied with certain things you have been doing for years.

4. It will be up to each person to sort out his own purpose, why he came, what he wants to do.

5. As you find your "path", then you have but to manifest and bring it into reality.

6. Notebook:
   a. Write any difference you have noticed in your "feelings" about situations, goals, people, the world in general, over the past year.
   b. Have you felt dissatisfied with your goals, your present employment, possibly things you have done for years? List these.

c. As you keep track of your "feelings", begin to categorize them. Categorize, date, and title them, day by day.

Prepare to make this a continuing project in your life. It only takes but a few minutes, but yet it will reward you with the answers you are seeking.

LESSON 35

Today is a day for celebrating, celebrating what you have accomplished thus far. You may believe what you have accomplished may not be much, but it is dear souls, because as you go along, it will grow. As things open to you, more will open and then more and more.

It is as though you go through a door and then there is another door to pass through and another. This is the nature of the way you will grow and learn.

Each experience, each learning experience, will precipitate another and yet another. It unfolds one by one by one. As each unfolds, you get a greater glimpse of "you", of what you have come to accomplish, of your relation to others and the rest of the world. So that say in a year's time, you look back and you will marvel at how far you have come and how you have grown.

In these learning experiences, will be the learning and the integrating, taking into your consciousness what these truths mean to you, fully, completely.

Dear friends, I will be with you during these processes, I will be with you to help you. I will be aware of each and every one of you reading this book and I will be here to help with your understanding and integrating.

Please remember you are parts of the whole, and as such, you may help your fellow souls. As I have asked you to see yourself connected with them, please do this often, because in so doing you are helping in their learning and understanding process also.

By thinking and connecting with your fellow souls, you send them energy and light to help them at whatever stage they are.

When all souls realize and believe and are able to fathom that all were meant to be a cooperating whole, your earth plane, as you know it will change in every way.

If you stop now and think, think of each person cooperating with the other, cooperating with the plant kingdom, animal kingdom, geological kingdom, can you imagine what a wonderful place your earth plane would be, your lives, your employment, how all would accelerate for the good? It would magnify, amplify. It may be hard for you to imagine this, because you have never experienced it, but dear souls, this is the way it was meant to be, all working and cooperating, one with the other.

Do you realize this is how we work in our realm, all for the good of each other and the whole? Each doing their part and in their own way for the total good of all? You are not a stranger to us, no, you are one of us, for we have met many times. These truths that I have conveyed to you are not foreign to you, because your soul knows them, your soul is well aware of them.

What I have tried to accomplish is the beginning of your learning process, your opening, as it were, to the learning process, your alignment with your soul, taking fully into your conscious mind what your soul already is aware of. Uniting it as one so that your conscious mind and your soul work together as one, not each separate as to itself. This is what I come to accomplish.

All are very separate, very unique, as I have stated before, but yet part of the whole.

As more and more open to their knowingness, they facilitate the opening of the others.

Everything is reciprocal, dear friends, everything. It is a give and take cooperation and love each for the other.

I would like you to think of all the other parts of the whole, often, and with love. In that way know that you will be helping them, helping them at whatever stage of growth they may be in.

This week dear friends is a time to think back over your accomplishments. Look back over how far you have come and at the same time realize this is just the beginning, your *new* beginning, the beginning of your evolvement.

Think back over the lessons. You may want to look over some of the past lessons in the book, remembering and realizing the progress you have made, then fully realize this is just the beginning, the beginning of your evolvement.

So for this week I would ask that you review and contemplate what you have learned, the way it has effected your life, and with anticipation contemplate what is yet to come.

Summary

Lesson 35

1. Today is a day for celebrating what you have accomplished thus far.

2. I will be aware of each and every one of you reading this book and I will be here to help with your understanding and integrating.

3. By thinking and connecting with your fellow souls, you send them energy and light to help them at whatever stage they are.

4. These truths that I have conveyed to you are not foreign to you, because your soul is well aware of them.

5. Think of all the other parts of the whole, often, and with love, in that way you will be helping them.

6. Please review and contemplate what you have learned thus far. Realize how far you have come and the progress you have made. This is your *new* beginning, the beginning of your evolvement.
   Look forward and anticipate what is yet to come.

7. Notebook:
   Write down and list how you believe this book has effected your life thus far.

Look back over how far you have come and at the same time realize this is just the beginning, your new beginning, the beginning of your evolvement.

LESSON 36

You are each one separate as to yourselves and still part of the whole, and as you realize this and take it into your being and contemplate it, many many things should begin to make sense to you.

As you go along, more and more during your quiet times and even at times during the day, things may pop into your mind, as a "light bulb flashing on" and more and more will make sense to you and become a part of your being. I cannot emphasize enough, the importance of taking the time I have asked to integrate and practice.

Many of the things you will read, will be counter to things you have learned. They may surprise you, shock you, disturb you, and yet you still may seem to have a consuming desire to know more. It is only human nature to question, to search, to attempt to rationalize and put everything in safe secure little pockets.

As you grew, when you were young, you learned many things. You learned in school, you learned from example and many of you learned from religious training. You grew up "programmed" I will call it, in certain ways. This program, is the way you think and act. It comes from the program of beliefs and things you learned while growing up.

These make up a stable "home base", I will call it, a base that is always there for you. You are familiar with this base, familiar and secure. You are secure in the knowledge that you believe and act on certain fundamental things that have become "home base", let's say.

As you go through life, you react to all things, from this base of beliefs and knowledge that was established long ago and added to little by little.

Of course each person is different because they were raised differently, have different personality traits and different reasons they came.

When you desire to know more, and you may question one of these basic beliefs, many times it is a "mixed bag" as you might say. You may be intrigued, curious and uneasy at the same time.

You may feel your "home base" shaken, because you rely on this "home base", it is more or less your "security blanket". When you begin to learn and question something new, that may be quite different than you have believed in the past, you need time for this new belief to "settle in".

It is a two fold process 1. It is the questioning and the wanting to know. 2. Then it is the acceptance of the fact and the "settling in". The "settling in" is what I refer to as integrating.

You each and every one have free will. You are free to pick and choose what you each want for your truths, your way of life, your beliefs. No one has the right to force these on you. It is your choice and yours alone.

Your beliefs and your actions should correlate. In other words you should not project to the outside world you believe one way, and yet act out opposite beliefs. This is hypocrisy. Hypocrisy is only living a lie, hurting yourself and setting a bad example for others.

The way of your beliefs should correlate with who you are, through and through.

In this way only can you align with your self/soul.

I have mentioned many times, the integration process, and how important it is that you spend a week on each lesson. I also realize that due to human nature, being what it is, many will try to skip ahead believing the lessons are too simple and easy for one week's duration. If you do this, you will end up only hurting your own learning and integrating processes.

As I stated in the beginning of this book, not to skip ahead and to make certain you spend a week's duration on each lesson, it was because I have written this book for beginners, those who are just beginning to question and learn what world evolution means to them. Those who want to learn a "path" to follow toward world evolution, so that it may happen, smoothly and without incident.

I hope you will have followed my instructions, for if not it is likely you will have to return to the pages and repeat the exercises I have laid out.

The lessons I have laid out are meant to build one on the other, giving you a good firm foundation. With this book and this firm foundation, you can then proceed on to further learning.

Know that I am a "teacher", dear souls, and as such "teaching" is my specialty. I write books and lay them out in a specific manner for very specific purposes. It all is for different, varied and specific reasons.

So in summary, this book has been arranged:

1. For simplicity and ease of reading (so that all, no matter what walk of life, no matter what education, they may read and understand)

2. Each lesson builds one on the other, giving time for integration and learning.

3. There is more meaning behind the words, than you can see (in other words it is written in a way to facilitate the learning process)

What I am asking this week is to review your lessons. If at this time you have skipped ahead and not spent the time that I have asked, I would ask you now to please go back and do so.

For the others who have spent the amount of time prescribed, I would ask that they review, thumb back through the lessons, contemplate the lessons they feel "drawn" to. You will feel "drawn to" the lessons that you may need a little more work on.

This will be the homework for this week.

Summary

Lesson 36

1. It is only human nature to question, to search, to attempt to rationalize.

2. You grew up "programmed", a program of beliefs and things you learned while growing up.

3. Your "home base" is this program of beliefs and knowledge that was added to little by little.

4. As you question and learn, at times you may feel this "home base" shaken, until the new belief is accepted and integrated.

5. Your beliefs should correlate with who you are, through and through. In this way only can you align with your self/soul.

6. As I have spoken of the importance of integration, if you have not taken the prescribed time, please take the time to review now.

7. For those who have spent the time, I would ask to thumb back through the lessons, and review those they are "drawn to".

8. Notebook:
   a. List the times you feel your "home base" was shaken and the learning of what truth that caused this.
   b. What were your feelings at the very first? What are they now?
   c. Do you feel you have integrated this into your "home base"?
   d. List any truths you feel you are not yet comfortable with, and date them.
   e. At a later time you may desire to return to these items, date and write how you feel about them at that time. In this way you begin to realize how much you have learned and grown since the beginning of this book.

LESSON 37

As you are separate unto yourselves and yet still a part of the whole, you function at a level of consciousness that may be different in each of you.

As you grow and develop spiritually, your consciousness changes. It changes so that it may take in more, it is more expansive, in a manner of speaking.

You may picture your consciousness similar to a round red ball. You see this round red ball, it is there before you. It is round, it is red and you may see the material it is made of, but you do not see, nor usually consider, all the other aspects of this ball.

In other words you do not consider how it was manufactured, the people that helped manufacture it, the many processes it went through in the manufacturing, what went into the making of the materials in the ball. You see what is in front of you, a ball, a red ball.

This is the way most people view themselves. You view "you", as *you*, what you see and what you have lived and accomplished on the earth plane during this lifetime.

Yet there are many other parts of you. You had previous lifetimes and learning experiences and they are a part of you also, you just do not realize it on a conscious level. They dwell in another level of consciousness, you might say, but they help make up a part of the "you" that is here in this lifetime.

You have had many learning experiences, many, and the "you" you are today, reflect these, whether you realize it at a conscious level or not. So that when you were born into this lifetime, you brought with you many experiences of what you would call "the past". They are with you in your soul memory, and your learning experiences of this lifetime are adding to your past experiences and lessons.

Do you see that as you have gone through your lifetimes, the lessons, the experiences have been many, and from all those experiences you are the totality of the "you" of today. What you may have lacked in one lifetime, you have attempted to rectify in another. But always you were learning, growing, moving ahead. Because you all have free will, you moved ahead at different paces.

Some have had many lifetimes and others few.

Your free will and choice have all to do with this, because you alone choose what you want in every way.

As I told you earlier, you make and create your own reality in every manner. However your life is, at this very moment, you have created it, for some specific reason that is your own. You may have had some lesson you wished to learn or some specific purpose to complete.

You alone have the power to change your life in every way and you are responsible for your life in every way.

This dear souls, you must realize. There are no outside forces determining your future, it is you.

You have every power you will ever need. You are self-sufficient unto yourself. If you are not satisfied with your reality as you see it today, in the next moment you have the power to begin to change it.

During the time and days that lie ahead, humankind will begin to learn their once forgotten powers.

Instead of hard physical work, stressful, pressured jobs, they will learn to work more with their true capabilities. They will learn to work on an "inner level" first, so that much efforting is done away with.

As you grow spiritually and expand your consciousness, as you begin to work on an "inner level" with people, situations and events, your life will be more abundant, joy filled and worry free. All these things are completely up to you, dear friends, because you have the choice, the choice of each and every thing in your lifetime and beyond.

You can choose to grow spiritually and expand your consciousness, or you can choose not to. It will be up to each and every one, which reality they choose. It is that simple.

This week I wish you to contemplate "you". Contemplate on the fact that you have lived many lifetimes to get to the totality of what you are today.

The "you" you are today, has been through many lessons and learning experiences. Although you may not recall these past lives, they are there within your soul memory and help to make up the "you" of today.

Contemplate the fact that you make your own reality, you choose your own reality in every way, then contemplate what reality you may want in the future. Don't effort, don't push, let it flow and during the week write down any feelings that may surface.

Summary

Lesson 37

1. As you grow spiritually, your consciousness changes, so that it is more expansive, and can take in more.

2. The totality of the "you" today, is made up of the many experiences throughout your lifetimes.

3. As you begin to work with people, situations and events on an "inner level", your life will be more abundant, joy filled and worry free.

4. It is completely up to each and every one, which reality they choose.

5. During your "quiet time":
   Contemplate the "you" of today.
   a. Contemplate the fact that you have lived many lifetimes to get to the totality of what you are today.
   b. Fully realize that you make your own reality, choose your own reality in every way.
   c. Ponder what reality you may want in the future.

6. Notebook:
   Write down any "feelings" that surface during the
   week.

LESSON 38

Y ou on the earth plane, at this very time, have the greatest chance of all. When I say that, I mean the greatest chance many have had for eons, the chance to end the cycles of reincarnation.

You my friends, each and every one, are there at this special time, for a special purpose. It is because you wanted to be, had a fervent desire to be. Although you may not realize it consciously, it is so. It is no accident you are here at this time.

It has been my purpose throughout this book, to gently remind you, to gently jar that memory into your consciousness.

Each of you who have read thus far, are at a different stage in their life, because as I stated before, you are each and every one different, with different desires, personalities, purposes, even though still a part of the whole.

It has been my purpose to gently remind you of what is to come and the steps you need to take to begin preparing for it. As I have also related, it will come, just as sure as day follows night, it is approaching.

It can be a wonderful time for rebirth, for the unfoldment of abundance, love and harmony that the planet has not seen for eons.

It is your time, dear friend, your special time. A special time in your own evolution, the evolution of your soul. It is not a time to dread nor a time to look forward to with fear. It is a time to look forward to with great anticipation and excitement, for you, your fellow souls and your planet.

You dear souls, are the children of the earth.

The children that have been through many lifetimes, experiencing, perfecting, growing. Now the time has come for this growth to bear fruit, the fruit of love, peace and harmony.

I cannot emphasize enough the importance it is to have love in your heart, because God is love, love for all.

As you look around, you see many in your world that you perceive as "much less than perfect". Unfortunately they are a product of their own processes. Know that each soul is trying to do the best that they can, at this very time.

This may seem an ambiguous statement, but it is true. Some are so mired in negativity, it is as a thick quicksand, and they cannot extricate themselves from it without help.

This is where you come in. Instead of hate for these people, they need love. When you think of these people, and you each know who they are, not only in your immediate lives, but world leaders, send them love. As you think of them with hate, it only slows their process to help themselves, and your world.

When you begin to realize you are all a part of the whole and connected, and that what each of you do effects the other, you have the beginnings.

To help your world today, during your quiet time, send out love to the world and it's peoples.

As you think during the day of peoples you may dislike, world leaders and situations you may abhor, if hate enters these thoughts, stop, pluck it out, throw it away, dispose of it and replace it with love.

See light as symbolizing love. Visualize a beam of light from you to that person, situation, country. Send love dear souls, because love conquers all. Many of you have read this in your bible and it is so. Love conquers all.

This is the key to the kingdom, you might say, because love produces love and it is as a snowball, the more love, the more it creates.

This my dear friends is what will bring about the evolution of your planet, the rebirth, wondrously, gloriously, through peace, love and harmony.

I would ask that each and every one of you keep this in mind and attempt to live your life in this manner. As I say this, I want you to realize there is always justice. I do not ask that you remain in some intolerable situation nor put up with a fellow man's injustices. I do not say this.

What I do say is to try to resolve situations and relationships with love. Work on an "inner level" first. You will come to a point, and you will recognize this point, at which time to go beyond, you are wasting your precious time and energy.

You do not need to tolerate others injustices against you, because you always have the choice to walk away. If you walk away, if there is no way they can produce their end result, then their game cannot be completed.

When you walk away, please try to think back on them and the situation with love. I understand and realize this may be very difficult in many instances. I understand this, but I also ask you to please make this effort.

Use your visualization processes and send them your beam of light, of love. Hate, contempt, dislike, never helped any situation, event, nor individual. It will only make it worse in every way. It will only make it unsolvable in every way.

Love is what will conquer all, dear friends, in the end, love will conquer all and lead to the rebirth, so long awaited.

This week I would ask that you practice this, during your quiet time and your waking hours. If you catch yourself thinking with extreme dislike, hatefulness, negativity toward a person, event, relationship, stop, pluck it out and replace it with love. Pluck it out and let that spot fill with the golden beam of God's love.

This accomplished, then send your beam of love to this person. As you are all part of the whole, it will be received. Rest assured, it will be received and in that way you grow spiritually and you help that person.

You may desire to keep notes in your notebook as to how many times you do this each day and with whom or what situation. This may give you an insight into many things.

Summary

Lesson 38

1. You on the earth plane now, have the greatest chance of all, the chance to end the cycles of reincarnation.

2. You are there, each and every one, for a special purpose.

3. You are the children of the earth, and now the time has come for your growth to bear the fruit of love, peace and harmony.

4. To help your world today, send out love to the world and it's peoples.

5. This week:
   a. During your "quiet time" send out love to the world and it's peoples.
   b. See light as symbolizing love. Visualize a beam of light from you to that person, situation or country.

   During your "quiet time" and waking hours:
   a. If you catch yourself thinking with extreme dislike, hatefulness, negativity, toward a person, event, relationship, stop, pluck it out and let that spot fill with the golden beam of God's love.

b. This accomplished, then send your beam of love to this person.

6. Notebook:
   a. Jot down in your notebook how many times each day you do this, with whom or what situation.

LESSON 39

What more could you ask, than to have God within, within each and every one of you.

You are God's children and as you have learned, created in his likeness. Created in his likeness is a broad statement and it has given rise to many questions. Questions such as: Do we look like God? Does he look like us?

Dear souls, God has many faces and that statement is meant to mean that God is within you, each and every one. You are he and he you, and in so being you can accomplish all things.

During the course of this book I have not only gently attempted to jog your memory on why you have come, I have attempted to jog your memory on the many capabilities you have, your powers, as I have referred to them.

The more you fully realize what these powers are, how they apply to each and every one of you, and the more you use them, the more they will grow. This is so, dear friends.

To use your powers, you must fully comprehend you are capable of it. Once you begin to use them, your expertise, let us say, will grow. Your energy will grow. You will grow in every way, because "you" will be in alignment with your soul and how you were created.

Humans have been at odds in this way for many many years.

All the wonderful capabilities you have, that make life joyous and abundant, you have denied.

It is ironic when you stop to contemplate this. All these capabilities have lain dormant all this time.

There was no need for wars, suffering, dissent, struggle, bitterness, because you each and every one had the capabilities within to overcome these and live an abundant, joyful life.

This week dear friends I would wish you to contemplate your powers. Return to some of the pages and review. Contemplate the ways in using your powers, as I have described them, contemplating the future, with the use of these powers.

I intend to go into the use of these further in a following book.

You are each and every one so special, so unique and I want this to fully sink into your consciousness. You have everything at your fingertips here and now, to change your life in every way.

You are a living miracle, you might say. Even the capabilities we have discussed, are only the tip of the iceberg.

As you learn and grow, you will be amazed at what you are capable of, with ease and joy. These are the things your soul knows, knows in it's divine memory. These things I come to make you aware of, aware that you have them and the ways to use them.

This is a short lesson, because I would prefer that you do some reviewing. Review and contemplate, contemplate your powers and capabilities. Realize they are truly yours and you can put them to work immediately for you. You can turn your life around, starting today, if you desire it and if you follow through on the things I have taught.

You can not only change your world around, but you can begin to change the world, with your thoughts and actions.

You can help others by sending them loving thoughts, helping them to go higher.

As I have stated, more than once, this is what it takes to change the world, all helping, cooperating together. All working toward the wonderful and loving rebirth of your planet, together, each doing his own part, with love and joy.

Contemplate your wonderful powers this week. During your quiet time, think how your life and the lives of others can be improved, changed for the good, with these powers.

Write down in your notebook your ideas and impressions. The next day you might review these and add more to your list.

Summary

Lesson 39

1. You are God and he you, and in so being can accomplish all things.

2. To use your powers, you must fully comprehend you are capable of it.

3. You are each and every one so special, so unique, I want this to fully sink into your consciousness.

4. As you learn and grow, you will be amazed at what you are capable of, with ease and joy.

5. During the week, review and contemplate:
   a. Your powers, realize they are truly yours and you can put them to work immediately.
   b. You can help others by sending them loving thoughts, helping them to go higher.
   c. Think how your life and the lives of others can be improved and changed for the good.

6. Notebook:

Write down your ideas and impressions.

Review the next day and add more to your list.

You are God and he you, and in so being can accomplish all things.

LESSON 40

My dear friends, it seems just yesterday we began this book, you and I, for I have been with you, each and every one.

We have covered much and you should have by now, a good fundamental background to work forward from.

As you learn of God's truths, his love, all the things that you are capable of, you will desire to know more, yearn to know more, and this is as it should be, because this is the way one grows.

It is not an overnight process, but a step by step process. A process of experiencing life while you go, experiencing and putting into practice the things I have taught you. Integrating, learning and experiencing, this is what it takes.

You learn as you go along, just as you learn from life experiences as you go along. As I stated earlier, I will be here with information for you, lessons for you.

With this book you have your beginnings and I mean just that, because there is much much more, and I will be here with the information to help you, teach you of universal truths and your part in your planet and in your universe.

It is a humble time, a time to realize what a small cog you are in the whole, but yet how separate you are each and every one and how necessary you are to the whole, each and every one.

I have discoursed much on all being parts of the whole, because this is one of the most important truths you must realize. In realizing that, taking it into your consciousness and living it, all things will fall into place and you will be enlightened more and more each day.

World evolution will not come about lovingly, by hate, distrust, wars, it will only come about by each person doing their loving part and by so doing, helping the others.

As more and more waves of energy reach your planet, and as more and more turn to love and cooperation, instead of hate and discord, more and more will be enlightened, uplifted.

As this happens, dear souls, your planet will be on the loving road to it's rebirth, the loving rebirth and regeneration.

Down through the ages much has been written regarding the period you now find yourself in. It has come from many sectors, your Bible, appearances of Our Lady and Prophets. They all tell the same story in their own way. Many have described probable realities, that are of a very negative nature, major earth disturbances, earthquakes, floods, and further, pestilence and disease.

These dear souls are all probabilities, because all have free will and may change or choose at any time. Probable realities are not to be dwelled on. Yes, in their day, these were warnings of probable realities that could happen.

Dear souls, as I have taught you, fear is one of the most destructive thought forms there is.

As you finish this book, I would wish for you to only think and dwell on the positive. Dwelling on the negative, the fear aspect, is a thing of the past. Let it slip into the past and be gone.

From this day forward, let only loving, positive thoughts enter. Make each day a joy to live, as it should be. As your thoughts turn to world evolution, let them see all parts of the whole connected, each to the other, in loving unity and cooperation.

Know that with your help, your living of your life in a positive loving manner, your visualization and help, that world evolution is on it's way. It is beginning and it will happen wonderfully, joyfully and lovingly, without incidence.

I would wish that not a day goes by, that you do not think, contemplate and visualize this. In so doing, dear friends, this is what you will be bringing about, you each and every one of you, in loving cooperation.

Please remember, every day of your lives, the God within you, the God who loves you, the God who has given you all good things.

Remember him, love him, make your soul a loving home for him, for he is within, waiting to be recognized and loved, waiting for you to begin to awaken to all the powers you forgot so long ago.

As we finish this book together, it is not the end, just the beginning.

The beginning of your planet's rebirth, the beginning of your evolvement and the beginning of all the information I wish to impart to you.

At this time I wish to thank you, each and every one, for following along as I asked, for the completion of your lessons and the time you have taken from your busy lives.

I would also like to thank my channel, who has so lovingly agreed to channel this information, through her, and get it out to the world.

I will return with more information in the next book of our series. Until that time, God be with you, each and every one. May you continue to grow, grow upwards and onwards toward the rebirth and regeneration of your planet.

Summary

Lesson 40

1. As you learn God's truths, his love, you will yearn to know more, because this is the way one grows.

2. With this book you have your beginnings. I will be here with much more information to teach you of universal truths and your part in your planet and in your universe.

3. As more and more turn to love and cooperation, instead of hate and discord, more and more will be enlightened, uplifted.

4. Fear is one of the most destructive thought forms there is.

5. Dwelling on the negative, the fear aspect, is a thing of the past. Let it slip into the past and be gone.

6. From this day forward, let only loving positive thoughts enter and visualize all parts of the whole connected, each to the other, in loving unity and cooperation.

Order Form

Postal Orders
Channel Publishing, 5942 Edinger, Suite 113-130
Huntington Beach, CA 92649

Qty	Item	Description	Price
		Subtotal	
		Sales tax*	
		Shipping	
		Total	

Sales tax:
Please add 6.5% for books shipped to California addresses

Shipping:
Book rate $2.00 for the first book and 75 cents for each additional book
(Surface shipping may take three to four weeks)
Air mail: $3.50 per book

Payment:
☐ Check   ☐ Money Order

Send to:

Name

Address

City   State   Zip